D1444541

THE GREY'S ANATOMY

Guide to Healing with Love

THE **GREY'S** ANATOMY

Guide to Healing with *Love*

with Dr. Sydney Heron

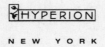

NEW YORK

The Grey's Anatomy Guide to Healing with Love
written by Chris Van Dusen

Grey's Anatomy © 2008 ABC Studios. All Rights Reserved.

Photography © American Broadcasting Companies, Inc.

This book is a work of fiction. The character, Sydney Heron, is a fictional character
from the ABC television show *Grey's Anatomy*. Therefore, Sydney Heron is not a
professional therapist and this book is not intended to be a substitute for professional
advice. All names, characters, businesses, organizations, places, events, and incidents are
imaginary and used fictitiously. Any resemblence to actual persons, living or dead,
events, or locales is entirely coincidental.

All rights reserved. No part of this book may be used or reproduced in any
manner whatsoever without the written permission of the Publisher.
Printed in the United States of America. For information address
Hyperion, 77 West 66th Street, New York, New York 10023-6298.

Library of Congress Cataloging-in-Publication Data is available upon request.

ISBN: 978-1-4013-0959-6

Hyperion books are available for special promotions, premiums,
or corporate training. For details contact Michael Rentas,
Proprietary Markets, Hyperion, 77 West 66th Street,
12th floor, New York, New York 10023, or call
212-456-0133.

FIRST EDITION

10 9 8 7 6 5 4 3 2 1

CONTENTS

FOREWORD

by Dr. Richard Webber

WHEN DR. SYDNEY HERON waltzed into my office and told me she was writing a book, I admit, I was a bit taken aback. First off, she hadn't made an appointment. Second, a *book*? Where did she find the time? I thought I was keeping my surgeons busy! The ferry accidents, the train wrecks, the bombs in the body cavities, the ambulance crashes—were they not enough? How on earth was one of my top senior surgical residents finding the time to pen, of all things, *a book*?

Then, I realized, this was *Sydney*. In all my years as Chief of Surgery at Seattle Grace Hospital, I've never met a doctor quite like Sydney Heron. Her graciousness, completely sincere. Her respectfulness, entirely genuine. Her eagerness, absolutely natural. And, of course, Sydney's loquaciousness . . . well, that's certifiably authentic.

It's true, Sydney likes to talk. Only because she has a lot to say. *A lot*. If anybody was going to write a book, if anybody *needed* to write a book, it was going to be Dr. Sydney Heron. The woman's seen some pretty nutty things. She's worked with some pretty wacky people. Look, she even invented her own life philosophy, complete with five principles and an official quiz. If *that* won't get you a publishing deal these days, then I don't know what will.

Dr. Heron calls her philosophy, "Heal with Love." From what I understand, it's learning to live in a way that allows you to conquer your fears, control your worries and overcome any challenge that life throws at you. According to Dr. Heron, you'll be able to let go of your issues, learn to forgive and ultimately accept yourself (as well as those around you) by investing in one thing and one thing only . . . *love*.

Now, there will be critics. There will be people who condemn Dr. Heron's so-called "philosophy." And, to tell you the truth, being a man of science, I wouldn't normally buy into the concept of "love healing all" either. However, I've witnessed Dr. Heron practice her philosophy firsthand, day in and day out. I've watched her extinguish many a fiery situation by simply "hugging it out." I've seen her counsel co-workers, console patients and inspire others with what Sydney calls, "pure, unadulterated, honest love." I won't say, for sure, that love heals all. But I will say that it can't hurt.

Not too long ago, I rescinded my plans for retirement. I was all set to throw in the towel on my job as Chief, but—on the day I was supposed to announce my successor—I just couldn't do it. Someone told me that I was *still* the best man for the job. I had the opportunity to do it all over again. From the beginning. *Differently*. I had the chance to learn from my mistakes. So, that day, I vowed to be a better Chief. A better husband. A better person.

This (I think) is what Dr. Heron means when she says that love is capable of healing all. Someone had enough love for me to make me realize the errors of my past ways. And I had

enough love for myself to listen to him. I'm still working on it—
this whole Chief thing. I'm still trying to do things differently.
I'm still trying to be better. But, as Dr. Heron will point out, it's
a journey . . . not a destination.

As Chief, I've grown accustomed to the fine art of reassuring
both patients and colleagues alike. I can't count how many times
I've told a worried mother that her son is "in good hands" here at
Seattle Grace. Or, how frequently I've encouraged one particular
doctor to be strong and keep her head in the game, after repeat-
edly finding her hiding in a supply closet. Moreover, I can't tell
you how often I've had to comfort a patient on the operating
table, right before he goes under . . . "You have nothing to worry
about," I always say.

Well, now I'd like to reassure *you*. It's you who are about to
turn the page and learn all about Dr. Heron's philosophy. I'd just
like to say that you're in good hands with Sydney. You're going to
have to be strong, though. The journey you're about to embark
on is not an easy one. Just try to keep your head in the game and
you'll be fine. Remember, in the end, you have nothing to worry
about . . . You're only up against yourself. Good luck . . .

INTRODUCTION

Healing and Love:
The Combo You Deserve

H EY, WHAT'S THAT SOUND? Over there, off in the distance. It's getting louder. It's getting clearer. I can almost . . . I think it's . . . encouragement! It sounds like—is that a little cheer? Why, yes, it's a congratulatory song of some sort! Can you hear it? Wait a minute, it's . . . it's meant for *you*!

Yes, *you*. Hearty congratulations to *you* are in order, my friend. Why? Because you picked up this book. You started reading it. You decided to take control of your life. You stomped your foot on the ground, stood proud and shouted to the high heavens: "I'm ready. I'm ready to heal with love!" And for that, boys and girls, I say to you: *Congratulations!*

You should be very proud of yourself, you know. All big and strong and, most importantly, open-minded. All ready to turn your life around and solve your problems with pure, unadulterated, honest love. I am so very excited for this journey we're about to take together. You and I. Me, Dr. Sydney Heron, and *you*. From this point on, I'm going to be your biggest cheerleader.

That's right, I'll be by your side helping you navigate the rocky terrain that life has built its lessons upon.

But, first, a warning. Well, it's more of a notice than an actual "warning." Okay, let me just get this out of the way: I am not a therapist. I didn't go to some fancy therapist school where I learned all the fancy things that fancy therapists know. I don't have a psychology degree or anything like that. No way, Jose! Let me say it again: I am not a therapist. But, I am a *healer*. I heal. I'm a doctor. And as a doctor, I've found that the best kind of medicine—the kind that heals all—is *love*.

So, why a book? Why did I decide to put pen to paper and write this extraordinary piece of literature? Well, I just told you the answer, silly. Because I'm a healer. Let me explain . . .

At Seattle Grace Hospital, that's where I work, I see so many people in need of love every day. My co-workers, my patients, my bosses . . . they're all in such desperate need of love. Each and every day, I stand by, sincerely pained, and witness people living their lives *tragically*.

They cut LVAD (Left Ventricular Assist Device) wires. They drown in very large pools of water. They go on one night stand binges. They hide their boyfriends' hand tremors. They sleep with their best friends. They get married in Vegas. They fall in love with Jane Does. They choose their jobs over their wives. They blame their husbands for leaving the baby gate open.

And I'm just getting started.

I've seen these kinds of problems up close and personal for a while now. At first, it was all very hard to watch. I found myself turning the other way every time an ex-wife from Manhattan showed up or pictures of a certain intern in her skivvies got posted all over the hospital. But you know, a healer can only play the silent bystander bit for so long. So, before I knew it, I found myself wanting to stand up and speak out. I found myself wanting—no, *needing*—to heal these people.

I remember, not too long ago, we had ourselves a bit of a situation at Seattle Grace. It was called a "Code Black." I wasn't too keen on that name, "Code Black." It just seemed to suggest imminent doom. It was almost as if something bad *had* to happen in order to live up to its daunting name, "Code Black." Anyhoo, a man came into the hospital with an actual bomb embedded in his body cavity! It was a serious situation to say the very least. One of our interns, Meredith, ended up sticking her hand inside of the patient because she thought the bomb was going to explode if she didn't do so.

Granted, maybe it was just the ill-fated term "Code Black" that propelled Mer's hand into that body cavity. The more likely force, however, was Mer's extreme case of *stinkin' thinkin'*. Without getting into specifics, this Meredith girl isn't exactly the brightest, shiniest girl on the block. But I bet if Meredith had learned to think more positively, and chosen to ignore all that "Code Black" hype, then she would've been a lot better off as she held onto that bomb lodged inside her patient.

I was really distraught over that whole fiasco. It seemed that everyone, not just Meredith, was thinking negatively. Talk about a bunch of wah-wah Debbie Downers! The only thing I could really do during that time was write down my feelings. It's important, you know, to talk about your feelings . . .

So, I started writing. I started to transform all of the negativity around me into something positive. I soon found myself listing the mistakes of those around me, and how I would venture to solve them if I were in their shoes. Here's what was funny: I noticed that all of my solutions shared a common theme: *love*. That's when it hit me—why keep all of this to myself? Why not share it with the world? Why not do what I do best? That is, *heal*. Gosh darn it, I could heal with love!

I realized that there are probably millions of Merediths out there, all needing to say buh-bye to their *stinkin' thinkin'* mindsets. There are probably trillions of people cutting LVAD wires, drowning in very large pools of water, bingeing on one night stands, hiding their boyfriends' hand tremors, sleeping with their best friends, getting married in Vegas, falling in love with Jane Does, choosing their jobs over their wives, blaming their husbands for leaving the baby gate open . . . Like I said, I could go on . . .

Well, I want to help and heal all of them. I want to help and heal all of *you*.

That's why I decided to write this book. Quite simply, I want you to learn from their mistakes. I want you to heal yourself as well as others. And, I want you to do so with love.

Because, let's face it, how does one heal after making a transcontinental booty call? With *love*. How about after failing a big test and having to repeat your intern year? You heal with *love*. Found a pair of panties that don't belong to you? Then heal with love! Poison oak on your va-jay-jay, ladies? Well, love heals all. Love, love, love!

I've really seen so much at Seattle Grace. And I've really met so many wonderful people. People with issues, people with problems, people with little quirks they have to work out, but *people*. People that need to learn how to heal with love. I'm going to tell you about all of them. And I really hope you can learn something along the way. Lord knows I have.

I'll begin with my five principles of healing with love. That's part one. Keep in mind, these principles didn't just evolve overnight. I didn't just wake up one morning and instantly know how to heal with love. No, siree. It took a good, long time to develop these beliefs. I've tested all of them, multiple times, in several situations. I think they do an extraordinary job of encompassing my entire heal-with-love philosophy. Study them. Learn them. Practice them. *Become* them.

In part two, you'll learn how to apply my principles, starting with relationships. There are so many kinds of relationships out there. Whether you're seeing McDreamy, The Ten-Year-Old, The Perfectionist, The Robot, The Husband Who Sleeps With His Best Friend, The Bad Boy or The ManWhore—I'll teach you how to survive relationships with each. And I'll teach you how to do so with those five principles you learned in part one.

Part three turns my attention to the most important person of all: *you*. The Big Kahuna! The cat's meow! The bee's knees! *You*. Part three was my favorite part to write because it's all about self-empowerment. Every issue, every personal problem, every *thing* can be solved with the healing power of love.

You'll notice that—throughout the book—I've taken the liberty of peppering in a few of my very own, tried and true, "Heronisms." These are simple daily exercises, affirmations and healing techniques. They'll help you practice my philosophy every single day for the rest of your life. Remember, practice makes perfect, my little students of love!

When you're done with the chapters, be sure to take the official Healing with Love Quiz, located in part four. Ace this, and you, my friend, are ready to put on your brave face, go out into the world and start healing with love!

So, come on! The train is ready to leave the station! The journey is about to begin! The keys to unlocking the secret healing power of love are just a page-turn away! Let's light a fire under that little tush and get you to turn the page!

PART ONE

The Five Principles of
Healing with Love

CHAPTER ONE

Love in the Present Moment

*"To change one's life: Start immediately.
Do it flamboyantly. No exceptions."*

—WILLIAM JAMES,
philosopher and psychologist

A IN'T THAT THE TRUTH! Not too long ago, Mr.
William James' very words changed my life infinitely.
They provided comfort and strength. Solace and peace. Vigor
and animation. Most importantly, those words provided me
with *hope*. Hope that, following an extremely difficult time, I'd
be able to pick myself up, wipe the dust off my blouse, begin to
move forward and start to *heal*.

You see, life wasn't always so lovely for Dr. Sydney Heron. I
wasn't always so . . . *together*. No, siree. I have a past. A little bit
of a history. A *story*, if you will. One that's not very pretty. There
was a time, if you can believe it, when I hit rock bottom. It was a
tremendously dark period of my life. A trying time when it literally felt like somebody punched me in my stomach, kicked me
down and held me there for a really long time, until all of the
life, love and hope drained right out of me.

But I'm not going to talk about that right now.

What kind of self-help book would this be if I started off

with the depressing times of one Sydney Heron? Not a very good one, I'll tell you that. Besides, you and I have plenty of time to get to the heavy stuff. We've just started to get to know one another. I don't want to make you go running for the hills and cryin' for your mama just yet.

Instead, I want to begin in a happy place. Doesn't that sound nice? A welcoming place filled with hope. Hope that—following whatever your current situation may be—you, too, can pick yourself up, wipe the dust off your blouse (or your shirt, gentlemen), begin to move forward and start to *heal*. Just like I did.

Mr. James' famous words can be directly applied to my healing with love philosophy. Healing, you see, evolves from change. I mean, the whole point of healing is to go from scary, damaged and broken to happy, bright and shiny, right? Well then, allow me to make a small revision to the aforementioned quote:

"To heal with love: Start immediately.
Do it flamboyantly, kinda."

—DR. SYDNEY HERON

Well would you look at that! Apparently, as you can see, Mr. James isn't the only one with the gift of gab.

In essence, my quote is telling you to love in the present moment. Well, say hello to our very first principle of healing with love: Seize the day! Carpe diem! Start immediately! And, do it flamboyantly! But, not *too* flamboyantly.

See, that's the trick. And that's where me and Mr. hoity-toity William James differ: An exception *does* exist. A major caveat comes along with Principle One. Allow me to explain . . .

By all means, you should seize every day of the rest of your life, starting *right now*. Treat every day as another chance for you to get your happy ending. Because, there really is no moment like the present to begin healing with love. Every day is another wonderful opportunity for you to begin that process. However, and that's a big, capitalized, italicized, even underlined *HOW-EVER*, there *is* such a thing as healing with *too much* love. It's easy to get to a point where you're living and changing and healing *way too* flamboyantly.

Healing with love, you see, is about moderation. My warning is simple: Choose to start healing with love right now. But, heal with *too much* love and you're going to get into trouble.

It's a fine line, really. And, my, my, my . . . I have seen *a lot* of people cross it. Time and time again, when people start on their heal-with-love journey, when they finally decide to start that process *right now*, in the present, they make the mistake of healing with too much love. It's a common pitfall. One that you need to be aware of if we're ever going to get you right.

Here's what I want to say if you find yourself using excessive love as a way to heal: It's not your fault. I know that. I've seen many people get caught on this little snare many, many times. The reality is, this book wasn't around when Meredith first stepped foot into the Emerald City Bar, was it? This book wasn't available at Addison's local bookstore before she made a transcontinental booty call, right? Well, it's okay if you, too, are making those same kinds of mistakes. As you read these very words, you're mastering Principle One. That's right, only number *one*! We have four more principles to go! I don't expect you to know how to *properly* heal with love quite yet.

Okay, let's see how this principle (and the caveat that comes along with it) works in the real world. Or, at least, how it works where I come from . . .

ONE STOP HEALING & ONE NIGHT STANDS

Once you've learned how to properly heal with love, you'll be equipped with a powerful tool. A weapon that will calculatingly destroy any unwanted fears, problems and sticky situations. But, we've just gotten started . . .

As we begin, you may suspect yourself of being someone who heals with *too little* love—a condition marked by feelings of sadness and regret. The majority of this book is devoted to helping you get out of that kind of rut. First, however, I'd like to focus on what lies at the opposite end of the spectrum. Something much more insidious. Something that you'll be tempted to do as you kick Principle One into fifth gear and start loving in the present moment. That is, healing with *too much* love—a condition that's pretty much marked by one thing and one thing only: The One Night Stand.

A one night stand is taking my first principle a little too far, don't you think?! Remember, *moderation. Balance.* Of course, love flamboyantly. But, not *so* flamboyantly that you have a one night stand with, say, every neurosurgeon that walks through the front door of your local bar.

Here are a few words to love by: A one night stand is *not* a form of healing with love. It's confusing, I know. But, a one night stand is just a sure, telltale sign that you are healing with *too much* love. A one night stand tells me that you are just a beginner! And, boy, you sure have a long way to go . . .

The truth is, you don't *heal* after having a one night stand. You certainly don't become the bright, shiny and happy person you're destined to be. Just trust me on this one. It's not that I've learned from direct experience. It's because I've seen *plenty* of colleagues attempt to heal themselves with love by having one night stands.

They were beginners just like you. I've learned from their mistakes. If you read carefully, you'll be able to do so, too.

Around here, there's a particular one night stand that everybody knows about. To this day, as a matter of fact, people are *still* talking about the consequences and ramifications of that infamous night. It happened between one saucy first-year intern and one brilliant neurosurgeon. I'm talking about Meredith Grey and Derek Shepherd, of course. Yes, *she* was just a simple, doe-eyed girl trying to survive Seattle Grace's intense, exasperating internship year. *He* was the hospital's newest hunky attending who seemed to make any girl who glanced at him swoon.

The night before Meredith's first day as an intern, the pair met at the Emerald City Bar, the watering hole across the street. Rumor has it that they soon went back to Meredith's place where they engaged in, you guessed it, a one night stand. The following morning, when Meredith arrived at her internship, she was shocked to discover that Derek was, in fact . . . her boss!

Meredith's problems were only beginning. She soon started to doubt her skills as a surgeon: Was Meredith scrubbing in with Derek because she was the best? Or was she scrubbing in with Derek because she had slept with him? Was Meredith getting special treatment? And, when the other doctors (myself included) found out about Meredith's relationship with Derek, those same questions were asked more and more often. Pretty soon, Meredith's one night stand started to affect *all* of her relationships.

Seattle Grace's most notorious one night stand made Derek's life a little more difficult, as well, you know. *Especially* when the Chief found out. That wasn't a very sunny day in McDreamyland, I can tell you that!

When Richard (that's our Chief) found out about Derek

sleeping with an intern, he was *not* a happy camper. No, he was not! Derek was the adult. Derek was the *attending*. Derek should've known better, the Chief concluded. So when Richard needed to appoint someone to act as Chief of Surgery while he recovered from a recent eye surgery (the poor thing), Richard chose Preston Burke, another Seattle Grace attending. That's right. He didn't pick Derek! Of course, Derek felt that he was passed over because he was sleeping with an intern. And, between you and me, Derek might've been right.

Now, do you see what I mean? All of those troubles, all of those problems, they all started because two people decided to have a one night stand. And what do we know about one night stands? Anyone? That's right, a one night stand is just a sure, telltale sign that someone is healing with *too much* love.

When that notorious one night stand went down, Meredith and Derek were, indeed, utilizing my first principle of healing with love. They were just doing it all wrong! The problem, you see, was that they were loving a little *too flamboyantly*. Yes, Meredith and Derek are the perfect example of the disastrous effects that oftentimes occur when you start healing with love: You heal with *too much* love! All semblance of balance and moderation flies out the window and you get into trouble! Double trouble!

So, why did Meredith and Derek attempt to heal with love on that fateful evening in the first place? What made them love a little too flamboyantly? What, exactly, made them take my philosophy's first principle to such an extreme level? Well, allow me to take a gander . . .

For those of you who don't know, Seattle Grace has one of the toughest surgical training programs in the nation. This place is no walk in the park, let me tell you. We don't just accept any ol', average Joe Schmo. You've got to be smart. And tough.

You've got to be skilled. And strong. You've got to have surgery in both your heart and your blood.

That describes Meredith to a tee. *Especially* that last part: "You've got to have surgery in your blood." Meredith is smart, tough, skilled and strong. She's a fantastic surgeon. She has surgery in her heart. And, she definitely has it in her blood—her mother is Ellis Grey, after all. A world-famous surgeon who once honed her craft in the operating rooms of this very hospital. As you can see, Meredith has a heck of a lot to live up to. My lord, does she ever!

So, in order to deal, let's just say Meredith isn't afraid of a little tequila. She's not scared of sleeping with inappropriate men, either. Derek wasn't the only one night stand of Meredith's life, you know. I could list them here, but I don't know if there's enough space. Okay, that wasn't very nice.

The point is, Meredith had several personal issues she was trying to get over when she took loving in the present moment way too far and decided to have a one night stand with Derek. Mommy issues, daddy issues, abandonment issues, intimacy issues, impulse control issues—*issues*, okay? Indeed, Meredith thought she was using love as a way to confront all of those issues. The problem, however, was that Meredith was using way *too much* love. And, it's this abundance of love that ultimately led Meredith down a path of self-destruction. I suppose this abundance of love leads *a lot* of girls down a path of self-destruction. While taking a stranger home may *feel* like you're healing some issue with love, it's only temporary. You'll soon discover— probably the next morning—that you're only contributing to the problem instead of healing it. Just something to keep in mind, ladies.

Now, Derek had a whole slew of issues that he was dealing with that night as well. No, he didn't have a famous surgeon as a mother. At least, I don't think he did. But what Derek did have . . . was a wife. A wife who cheated on him with his best friend, in his own Manhattan brownstone, on his own flannel sheets. You see, when Derek had a one night stand with Meredith, he was trying to heal a very real, very painful wound with love. That wound was called Addison.

When Derek arrived in Seattle, he was looking for a fresh start. A new beginning. Those are fun, new beginnings. And very necessary sometimes! Especially after you catch your wife and your best friend in a rather compromising position in your bedroom. So, what do you do? You take a job across the country at a fancy hospital and attempt to get over it. You meet a pretty young thing in a bar, take her home and have a one night stand. Look at you: Loving in the present moment, healing all your wounds with love. Right? Wrong!

You see, even brilliant neurosurgeons can misunderstand Principle One. So don't beat yourself up if you find yourself loving in the present moment a little too flamboyantly as you learn to properly heal with love. If smarty-pants neurosurgeons are unable to avoid the common pitfall of healing with *too much* love, then YOU are excused, too!

When all was said and done, that one night stand didn't fix Meredith's mommy issues, did it? Nope. She still had to live up to her mother's famous name even after she slept with Mc-Dreamy. And that one night stand certainly didn't just erase Addison from Derek's memory, now did it? I don't think so. Addison was still around and still present in Derek's life. She even moved to Seattle and had quite a few one night stands of her own.

Oh, yes, it's the sad truth. I'll get to the whole Meredith-Derek-Addison of it all later, but for now, I'll just focus on the one night stands. Oh my, Addison had a few of those bad boys back in her day. One even began with a transcontinental booty call . . . to *Mark Sloan*, of all people. Mark was Derek's best friend. That's right—the *same* best friend Addison cheated on Derek with . . .

After Addison was unable to win Derek back from Meredith (more on that later—it includes a pair of panties and gets *really* good), she picked up the phone, made one *very* long-distance phone call and summoned Mark to her hotel room. Clearly, Addison had *a lot* of open wounds to mend. When she made that call, she was just another person starting to heal with love. Addison was simply trying to practice Principle One. Trying it on for size, if you will. The operative word here, obviously, is *trying*. It goes without saying that Addison failed miserably . . .

Mark ended up moving to Seattle, too. That complicated *everyone's* lives, *exceedingly*. After bringing Mark out to Seattle for "just sex," Addison got a whole lot more than she bargained for. Mark meddled and got into everybody's business. He threw his hat in the race for the Chief's job. And, above all, Mark continued to torment Addison in particular. He diluted her mind with dreams of towel-wearing McSteaminess and sixty-day sex bets. In short, Mark's presence wasn't good for Addison. But, she *had* to do it, right? She just *had* to invite him to Seattle for "just sex." Well, she learned her lesson the hard way. Oh, Addison, you were healing with too much love, sugar.

Transcontinental booty calls and one night stands—they kinda go hand in hand, don't you think? They're classic signs of someone who's just starting to heal with love. Someone who clearly has a *long* way to go . . .

Hopefully, these examples show you what *not* to do if you're faced with similar situations. Moreover, they might offer you a bit of comfort, knowing that there are other people out there experiencing the exact same problems. I know you're all out there, dealing with your own neurosurgeon bosses or your cheating wives or your McSteamy fantasies. Well, as I hope I've started to make clear . . . you're not alone.

It's important to remember that, as you begin this journey, you'll probably be tempted to heal with excessive love, too. It's only natural. Hey, it's gonna take some time to achieve a *total* heal with love equilibrium. So, if you find yourself faltering, try channeling your energy into something constructive. Maybe it's a new hobby. Maybe you knit instead of having another one night stand. Knitting is fun. Knitting won't lead you down a path of self-destruction.

Or, the next time you've had a long day and suddenly find yourself in a bar, try saying no to tequila. Switch to the carbonated beverage of your choice. It's really easy, you'll see. I've found that club soda, straight up, tastes just as good as any alcohol I've ever tasted. And, if you want to be daring, squeeze a lime or two in there. Simply divine!

Of course, another way to avoid Principle One's common hazard is by becoming celibate. Just don't run into any handsome veterinarians and you'll be fine! Look, here's the thing: Just find something you love to do (other than sleeping with inappropriate people you pick up at a bar) and *do it*. Every day. Start immediately. And, do it flamboyantly (just remember, not *too* flamboyantly). Learning to heal with love doesn't happen overnight. It's going to take a lot of time, patience and discipline. So, if, at any time, you fall off the horse, just know that mistakes come with the territory. Take a breath and get yourself right back up into that saddle!

Loving in the present moment—seizing and taking advantage of every day—is *not* about having a one night stand. It's about managing whatever pain you're carrying around by loving *yourself*. Loving is living, people. The shotgun just went off! So, go ahead . . . Start to *love*. And, start to live.

HERONISM

Here's a way to kick-start your healing with love journey—write a haiku! Look, you've already taken the first step in learning my philosophy—you read Chapter One! Now, put your budding education into overdrive and construct a poem. This exercise will allow you to think about your current situation from an emotional stance. Here's an example:

> *behold the stranger*
> *in bed the morning after*
> *still lonely not healed*

Now, it's your turn! Your first line should contain five syllables, the second should have seven syllables, and the third—five syllables. It's important to convey some kind of emotion. Give it a whirl!

CHAPTER TWO

Say Buh-Bye to Stinkin' Thinkin'

*"Attitude is a little thing that
makes a big difference."*

—WINSTON CHURCHILL

IT'S BEEN CALLED many things: The power of positive thinking. The law of attraction. "The Sedona Method." "The Secret." "Chicken Soup for the Soul." I could continue, but I should really stop there. Why? Well, continuing with that lengthy list wouldn't be good for either of us. When I start thinking of powers and laws and methods and secrets and chicken soup, I just get confused. And hungry. That's not what I want to do for you, my little student. In fact, making you confused and hungry is the exact opposite of my goal in writing this book. I want to provide you with clarity and satisfaction. I want to provide you with the necessary tools that will allow you to heal with love. Remember? Happy, bright and shiny: *good*. Confused and hungry: *bad*. Plus, secrets, secrets are no fun. Secrets, secrets hurt someone. Sorry, just had to go there!

Okay, pop quiz!

Ah, didn't see that one coming, did you? I bet you didn't even know this book was going to be riddled with the occasional pop quiz. Well, it is. But, these quizzes are for your own good. They'll also prepare you for the Official Healing with Love Quiz at the end of the book. Now, don't get all worried. I don't want to stress you out. *Inhale.* Come on, deep breath. And . . . *exhale.* Good. Nobody said learning to heal with love was going to be easy. If it was so easy, then everybody would be doing it. If it was so easy, then I wouldn't be writing this book. Now, back to that pop quiz . . .

What do the following statements have in common?

A. "She now has my McDreamy and my McDog. She's got my McLife. And I've got . . . what?"
B. "A quiet board in the morning is a board shot to hell by noon. A quiet board means trouble. A quiet board is death. A quiet board bodes bad things."
C. "There's not going to be any baby born today. I can't. I can't do this without my husband. I can't do this all alone."
D. "Pink mist. A bomb goes off and anyone within range explodes into a billion little pieces. You're liquid. Nothing's left. Pink mist. One minute, you're a person. And the next, you're bloody rain."

If you answered, "Dr. Heron, I believe those are all statements uttered by people exhibiting classic symptoms of stinkin' thinkin'," then you are indeed correct! You get the gold star of the day! Kudos to you!

Let's face it, we've all done our fair share of stinkin' thinkin'. I know I have. Working in a hospital, it's particularly easy to stink think. I mean, I'm working in an environment plagued by sickness. A place where bad news is told to loved ones on a daily basis. A location where people yell, "Code Black!" The scent of death is in the air around here. Oh my, would you look at that?

No, don't. Don't reread this paragraph. I'll admit it—I was just stinkin' thinkin'. See what I mean? We're all guilty of it!

This is going to be a difficult chapter to write. I literally have to transport myself to a dark place. I have to force myself to think back to not-so-happy times. And, that's not good. Oh dear, there I go again . . . I wrote, "And, that's not good." Classic stinkin' thinkin'. I guess I could erase it, but then, how would you learn? Anyway, never say something's not good. Rather, say you don't like something. It makes a world of difference.

Stinkin' thinkin' means thinking negatively about something. And, in order to heal with love, you need to say buh-bye to it. That's Principle Two. It's about taking control of your mind, rather than letting your mind take control of you. *You* and *only you* can change the way you think. You have a choice: You can think sad thoughts. Or you can think happy thoughts. You can think of dark skies. Or you can think of sunshine. You can reflect on what it means to evaporate into pink mist. Or you can ponder how much silkier your hair has become after switching to a certain lavender conditioner. Rain or rainbows? Weeds or flowers? Cockroaches or ponies? The choice is yours!

I suppose that choice really depends on whether you want to spend your life smiling or crying. When you think about that, you'd have to be a fool to pick the latter. Your thoughts can make you either happy or miserable. You put the same amount of work into both, so why not decide to be happy? Go ahead! Say buh-bye to stinkin' thinkin'!

Now, I'm all about shortcuts. If there's a quick and efficient way to get something done, then I'm game! I'll let you in on a little *secret* of my own: The quick and efficient way to say buh-bye to stinkin' thinkin'? *Love*. That's right. Love is the answer.

No one can argue that love is anything but a positive thing. Whether you love your boyfriend, your girlfriend, your husband, your wife, your friend, your bartender, your attending that allowed you to scrub in on an advanced procedure, or *yourself*—if you're loving, you're thinking positively. If you're loving, you're looking stinkin' thinkin' directly in the eye and saying that magical phrase: "Buh-Bye!" *This*, my friend, my student, my person *I* love, is what healing with love truly means!

Now, personally, I'm an optimist. I pick the happy thoughts—the flowers, the rainbows, the ponies, the lavender conditioner. You know, I once heard about the term "superoptimist." I like it. Has a certain ring to it. Clever. It's really true—there's not much use in being anything else besides an optimist. Take it from me! Or, take it from the story I'm about to tell you. A sad little story beset by a severe bout of stinkin' thinkin' by *all* involved parties. One that you can learn from. One that you yourself can *heal* from. Okay, here's what happened . . .

~~Code Black~~
Code Cloudy Skies with a 100% Chance of Afternoon Sunshine

I had just finished treating a patient's superficial wound when I got the page.

As a general surgeon, treating a superficial wound doesn't exactly top my list of all-time favorite pastimes. We surgeons prefer to be in the OR. Cutting. Operating. Saving a life. It's exhilarating stuff. But, you can't *always* be the lucky person who gets to scrub in. I mean, there are so many surgeons in a hospital and only a handful of operating rooms. You do the math.

Anyway, I was telling all of this to myself as I bandaged my patient's minor scrape. I wasn't going to partake in any stinkin' thinkin' that day. That superficial wound sure was enough to keep Dr. Sydney Heron occupied! I didn't need a really cool surgery to get me through what was shaping up to be an incredibly slow day. I didn't need to weasel my way onto a surgical case *yet again*. And I certainly didn't need to deal with the woman who had been screaming bloody murder in the middle of the ER *all morning*. No, siree! Besides, Alex, one of Dr. Bailey's interns, looked like he was handling the screaming lady all by himself.

Oh, that screaming lady. I'll never forget that sound. I believe her name was Mindy. She came into the ER with her husband moments earlier. She wasn't injured. She was just . . . screaming, I told you. She was in shock. Her husband, who seemed to have a pretty bad chest wound, was rushed to a trauma room. Here's what I remember the most about the husband: A paramedic had her hand literally stuck inside of the patient's chest. Yes, the paramedic's arm was inside that man's body cavity! It was the strangest thing. I guess she was trying to stop the bleeding, but you *never* put your hand inside a patient's body cavity. They moved past me so fast. All adrenaline. Full steam ahead! But, I had my superficial wound, which, you know, was FINE with me.

Alex eventually got the screaming lady to stop screaming. He decided to fight fire with fire on that one. Alex got in Mindy's face and screamed right back at her! Well, it worked. Because, finally, Mindy seemed to quiet down.

Soon after, another surgical case slammed into the ER. This patient's name was Tucker. He had apparently been involved in a car accident and now had a major head injury. Sounded like a case for Derek, our star neurosurgeon. He'd probably need to perform some really cool, extremely educational surgery, but, you know, I was just about to send my superficial wound guy on his way home. And, I told you, that was FINE with me!

So, like I said, *that's* when I got the page. As my pager buzzed, my mind started to wander . . . Who had been thinking of me?

Who sent me this page? Maybe they needed an extra set of hands for nasty chest wound guy. Maybe it was Derek himself, needing some advice regarding Tucker's pending operation. I could be scrubbing in after all, I thought! Yes, happy things flowed through my mind as I picked up my buzzing pager. I scrolled through . . . And, read something that I totally did not expect: "CODE BLACK!"

Code Black?

That's what the page said, Code Black. I remained calm, met my interns in the locker room, informed them of the Code Black situation, and told them they needed to evacuate the hospital. Immediately. That's what Code Black usually means. Evacuate. In this case, as I soon discovered, it meant: Evacuate because we have a bomb in a body cavity.

I realized that the paramedic I had seen earlier had her hands on live, unexploded ammunition in nasty chest wound guy's body cavity. The bomb squad was called in and it was determined that the east surgical wing was the only part of Seattle Grace that was in danger. No one could go near there. Since we didn't have to actually evacuate the entire hospital, I stayed in the lobby area and *prayed*. If there was ever a time for happy thoughts, that was it.

Derek, Burke, Meredith and Cristina were still up there! They were my people! You know, I was seated next to Derek at an M & M once. I learned alongside Burke when we treated a case of flesh-eating bacteria. I had the pleasure of being Meredith and Cristina's temp resident when their normal resident, Dr. Bailey, needed to go on bed rest. I *knew* them! They were my friends!

What's worse is that I soon learned that *Meredith* had somehow replaced the paramedic and put her own hand in nasty chest wound guy's body cavity! There was a bomb in a body cavity and

Meredith had her hand directly on top of it! There was absolutely no room for any stinkin' thinkin' *whatsoever* at that point.

Oh, and Tucker? The Tucker that had suffered from a bad head injury after he was involved in a car accident that morning? Well, that Tucker turned out to be *Bailey's* Tucker! Bailey's *husband*! He was caught up there, too. Bailey—who was about to deliver her baby—probably didn't even know her husband was in the hospital.

So, I *prayed* harder. I thought even *more* positively. The flowers, the rainbows, the ponies, the lavender conditioner? That wasn't enough! I needed to go to the unicorns, the butterflies, the happy little puppies that gleefully roamed the countryside behind their mama. I wasn't going to let stinkin' thinkin' rear its ugly little head in my mind. No way, no how.

And then the bomb went off.

It was like a shock wave. My stomach dropped. My skin started to tingle. My head started to feel light. But I pushed through and remained committed to thinking positively. Everyone around me was okay. I kept my spirits up. I raised my sights. I visualized the happy endings. Good fortune, I thought, surely shied away from gloom.

As for my friends upstairs . . . They were going to be fine, too. I just needed to wait for them.

And, as I waited—as *we all* waited—time felt like it stopped on a dime. It felt like several hours were passing when, in reality, it was only a matter of minutes. The elevator dinged. Out stepped Derek and Burke. They told us the news . . . Everyone— Derek, Burke, Meredith, Cristina, Tucker, nasty chest wound guy . . . Everyone was fine. Everyone except Dylan, the bomb squad expert. Unfortunately, Dylan passed when the bomb exploded.

I send sincere condolences to all of Dylan's family.

To put it mildly, that was *not* a good day. However, we must remember, even though *every* day may not be good, there will be *something* good in every day.

Let's take a moment to think about the *good* things of that day. Bailey had a healthy baby boy. Mindy got to see her husband again. Both Derek and Burke got to see their girlfriends again (Meredith and Cristina, respectively). Yes, some people learned just how much others meant to them. Relationships were strengthened. Friendships were made. Many, many happy endings prevailed.

Now, I'd be foolish to think that my thoughts of unicorns, butterflies and puppies made all of that happiness possible. They didn't. What they did do, however, was help me through an extremely intense, emotional time. My friends could have died. *I* could have died. Yes, it's very true. That bomb could have destroyed the entire hospital. Nobody knew for sure. I could have DIED. So, I basically had two choices: I could either get through that day with a positive attitude. Or, I could end without one. I think I made the right decision.

In essence, as I sat in that lobby with my unicorns, butterflies and puppies, I was healing with love. I was healing *myself* with love. I really wish more people had jumped on the heal with love bandwagon that day. Things would've gone quite differently if they did . . .

For one thing, Meredith started off her day stinkin' thinkin'! I mean, really, Meredith didn't even want to go into work that morning. Everything was all "bad feelings" and "thoughts of death" and "boyfriends choosing their wives" and "giving away McDogs" and "trading McLives" and CRY ME A RIVER, MEREDITH! Nobody should begin her day like that. Because, where did all of that negative energy get Meredith? *Exactly.* To an operating room where she had her hand stuck in a body cavity. *On a bomb!* Meredith? Positive anything is better than negative thinking. Somebody should've told her that.

I could say the same thing to Richard too. Remember, Richard is our Chief of Surgery. He started off his day being spooked by a "quiet board." Oh, the statements I heard come out of Richard's mouth that morning were *awful*. Rather, I should say, I didn't like the things that came out of Richard's mouth that morning. He said a quiet board bodes bad things. Really, Richard? Bad things like Bailey's husband getting into a car accident and needing brain surgery? Bad things like live, unexploded ammunition lodged in a man's chest? Bad things like having to evacuate half of your hospital and declaring a Code Black? Of course it was all doom and gloom that day! Misery is one of the worst communicable diseases out there! And, on that particular day, Richard might've been the person who needed to be treated for that kind of sickness the most.

Likewise, when Bailey found out about her husband's car accident, she started spewing all kinds of stink think. She said she couldn't have her baby that day. She couldn't do it without her husband. She couldn't do this, couldn't do that. Couldn't? I'm not very fond of that word. Lucky for her, though, one of her interns, George, was in the room. It was up to George to convince Bailey that she *could*. George, he's one of my favorites. He had a great, positive outlook on life that day. He coached Bailey through the delivery and, before they knew it, little baby Bailey was born! Know why? Because attitudes, both good and bad, are contagious! And, George's good attitude helped Bailey deliver her baby boy.

On the flip side, it was a certain anesthesiologist's *bad* attitude that caused quite a mess. It was that doctor's thoughts about "pink mist" that permeated our paramedic's mind, causing her to negligently remove her hand from her patient's body cavity and flee the scene. Ultimately, it was the anesthesiologist's thoughts that caused Meredith to put her hand on a bomb in a body cavity. And, well, you now know how the story ends.

None of those people were thinking positively. Even more alarmingly, none of those people were thinking about loving. Don't forget that the quickest way to say buh-bye to stinkin' thinkin' is with *love*. Sadly, not enough people chose to love that day. Not enough people picked the good thoughts over the bad ones. What a shame . . .

A friend of mine once told me: "When you feel dog tired at night, it's probably because you've growled all day long." It's the truth—stinkin' thinkin' is exhausting. It certainly made for a pretty extraordinary day at Seattle Grace, didn't it? The bad thoughts—the bad feelings, the quiet boards, the can'ts, the pink mists of the world—all of those things are insidious traps. Remember though, it takes just as much energy to fall into those traps as it does to climb out of them. Ultimately, the choice is yours! You can be happy. Or, you can be sad. You can think about your bomb in a body cavity. Or, you can think about your lavender conditioner. Take it from me—*always* choose the lavender conditioner. You'll be happy you did.

CHAPTER THREE

Appreciate Appreciation

"God gave you a gift of 86,400 seconds today.
Have you used one to say 'thank you'?"

—WILLIAM A. WARD,
author

QUESTION: WHAT IS GRATITUDE? Go ahead, take a moment to really think about it. Is it a feeling? An emotion? A virtue? Is gratitude simply saying "thank you"?

"*Thank you*, Derek, I would be honored to scrub in on your craniotomy."

Is gratitude counting your blessings? Is it being aware of the kindness of others?

"Why yes, Derek, it really is a beautiful night for saving lives. *Thank you* for that encouraging sentiment."

Can one even define gratitude? Is it even possible?

Well, for the purposes of this book, gratitude is an attitude. Let me rephrase that—gratitude is the *best* attitude. It's a way of life. It's a state of mind. It's all of the above, really. It's also Principle Three in a nutshell.

Surgeons are wired to think quickly and critically in the OR. We cut. We clamp. We suture. When complications arise, we know what to do. We assess the situation. We make the right decisions. We spring into action. And, hopefully, we save a life.

Whether we have a woman with a 65-pound tumor on the operating table, or we're elbow deep in a man with a major teratoma on his belly—our quick and critical thinking is second nature. We can't help but do everything we possibly can to save a patient's life. It's an innate, uncontrollable urge and desire that all of us surgeons have in common.

Well, I want you to view gratitude as that same kind of innate, uncontrollable urge and desire. I want those feelings of thankfulness and appreciation to be second nature to you, just like quick and critical thinking is second nature to surgeons. Mastering Principle Three will allow you to say the following phrases. Moreover, saying the following phrases will allow you to master Principle Three:

"I can't help but say 'thank you.'"

"I can't help but count my blessings."

"I can't help but appreciate the good things in my life."

"I can't help but feel grateful!"

If you can read this sentence, you can say "thank you." You're breathing. Thank your parents! You're able to read. Thank your teacher! You're able to purchase this book. Thank your boss or whoever else allows you to make an honest living (hopefully). There really is *so* much to be thankful for. Go ahead—give thanks. Say "thank you" to someone—say it to anyone. Just say it loud and say it proud because silent gratitude doesn't do anything for anybody.

Principle Three builds on Principle Two. Once you start appreciating, you'll discover you're thinking positively at the same time. They sorta go hand in hand. Not only are you thinking about the flowers, the rainbows, the ponies and the lavender conditioner, but, you're *appreciating* them as well. You choose to be grateful and you choose what to be grateful for. In essence, you're changing your perspective with Principle Three. You're changing your outlook on life. And, of course, you're healing with love in the process.

If you're appreciating everything you've got, then you're sure to appreciate everything you're going to get. And, trust me, once you begin appreciating the good things, more and more good things will come into your life. It's a scientifically proven fact! Well, not really, but I like to think so!

The truth is, *all* of us have something to be grateful for. I don't care who you are. Remember, much like thinking positively, gratitude is a choice. You can either thank the lucky stars you were named Chief Resident *or* you can hide in a supply closet wondering if your husband is cheating on you with a pretty model-turned-doctor. The choice is yours! You can either count your blessings or not . . .

Now, as for me, I count my blessings pretty regularly. Around here, I think of them more like "miracles." Ever since I started working in a hospital, I've been privy to many, many miracles. I watched Meredith come back to life after drowning in the Sound. I saw Cristina survive an ectopic pregnancy, Burke a gunshot wound. I witnessed Izzie and George pull themselves together after the tragic deaths of their loved ones. This entire hospital endured a Code Black and *I* lived to tell about it.

Oh, yes, I see all kinds of miracles—all kinds of blessings— every single day. My colleagues, my patients—they oftentimes face seemingly insurmountable odds. And they oftentimes overcome them . . . With the help of their friends, of course.

You see, a friend is one of the most glorious, most beautiful blessings of all. Friendship, I think, is perhaps the single greatest thing to be grateful for. Friends make you happy. They guide you through your darkest hour. They help you survive. When counting your blessings, when beginning to appreciate appreciation, start with your friends. Making a friend, as well as being a friend, means you're healing with love by its very definition.

It's okay to be thankful even if you have just one true friend. Appreciate him/her every single day. Once you start doing that, you'll find yourself appreciating everything else in your life. Those wonderful thoughts of appreciation will be second nature. You won't be able to help yourself from saying "thank you." You won't be able to help yourself from counting your blessings, from appreciating the good things in your life or from feeling grateful. Friendship is a force of nature. It really is! If you don't believe me, if you need proof, then pay attention to this next part . . .

Are You Somebody's Person?

Seattle Grace has proven to be fertile ground for developing some pretty solid, long-lasting friendships. For doctors, friends are particularly important. We work hard for our money around here, sometimes enduring shifts that last longer than forty-eight hours. So, we need friends to help us get through our tough days. We need friends to console us after life throws a curve ball. We need friends to help us survive. Perhaps even more importantly, we need to *be* a friend. We need to help others get through their tough days, too. A friend is truly one of the best things to have, and truly one of the best things to be.

I work with a particular doctor here who's known as a "tough cookie." Her name's Cristina and, based on my previous interactions with this co-worker, she is *not* exactly a people person. Yes, Cristina's pretty much the opposite of me. *I* love people. *I* love working with people. *I* love talking to people. *I* love trading secret family pie recipes and engaging in stimulating conversations on anything from favorite movies of the fifties to the protection of our endangered wildlife. Guilty! It's true! Anyhoo, my point is, unlike *me*, Cristina is a bit socially retarded, emotionally stunted, conversationally challenged—I mean, take your pick!

I've never really gotten along with Cristina. Rather, Cristina has never really gotten along with me. Our mutual problems stem from a case of flesh-eating bacteria we once worked on together. Without getting into the details, it was clear that Cristina didn't trust me on that case. In fact, Cristina made it clear, more or less, that she didn't care for me or my surgical skills very much. But, that's neither here nor there. To each his own, I suppose!

Still—ruthless, cutthroat, non–people-loving Cristina manages to have friends! Moreover—arrogant, presumptuous, overly aggressive Cristina manages to *be* a friend! To several people, in fact. How does she do it? Heck if I know! But, if Cristina can appreciate and count her blessing of friendship, then so can you!

It's been said that Cristina is Meredith's *person* and vice versa. Legend has it that "person" is derived from "emergency contact person." As in, the name of the emergency contact Cristina gave the clinic when she decided to terminate her pregnancy. Okay, "person" just means "friend." Meredith is Cristina's *friend* and vice versa.

Yes, when Cristina was pregnant with Burke's baby—after Cristina lost consciousness in the middle of the OR because of her ectopic pregnancy—Meredith was there for her friend, helping her survive. In fact, *all* of Cristina's friends were there for her. They all helped her recover. It's true—surprisingly enough—pompous, bold, way-too-ambitious Cristina has more than just *one* friend. Guess you just gotta love her, right?

I remember seeing a post-op Cristina, quietly lying there in her hospital bed after surgery, with all of her friends surrounding her. It was a magnificent sight! Meredith, George, Izzie and Alex—Cristina's *friends*—were there to support her. I recall passing the group and thinking to myself, "Now, *that* is a lucky girl." It was very touching and moving to see Cristina and her friends together.

That's probably the moment I realized that friendship isn't really a big thing. Rather, friendship is a million little things. It's the bond Meredith and Cristina started to form ever since the first day of their internship. It's the conversations they've shared about McDreamy and Burke at Joe's bar after a long shift. It's the way Cristina rubbed her friend's feet when Meredith was on the operating table after drowning in the Sound. All of those little things—and a million more—define their friendship.

Cristina and Meredith's friendship is one that's powerful and strong. Even though they'd never admit it (vocally, that is), Cristina and Meredith cherish each other like little treasures. Even though they don't enjoy talking about their feelings and crying about their problems while wearing pajamas—like *me*—they still manage to take care of one another. They're able to sit, without saying a word, and then walk away feeling as if *that* was the best conversation they've ever had. And that's a wonderful thing. In their own special way, Cristina and Meredith overcome obstacles *together*. They appreciate each other. They practice Principle Three. They are grateful. They heal with love and they *survive*.

There's another friendship around here that I need to tell you about. It's one that began long before Cristina met Meredith at Seattle Grace. This friendship comes from Manhattan. It's lasted years and has even survived a torrid affair. I'm talking about Seattle Grace's resident man-candy: McDreamy and McSteamy.

Derek and Mark. Now *that's* a friendship that has certainly had its ups and downs, let me tell you!

Here's a little back story on the two docs many of us here refer to as "pretty and prettier." Derek and Mark worked together back in New York. They were the best of friends. When Derek married Addison, Mark was the best man. All three of them, as a matter of fact, seemed to be very close. Yes, Derek thought of Mark like a brother. Until Derek found Mark in bed with Addison. So, Derek moved to Seattle to get away from all of the drama. And, Addison followed. And, of course, after that, Mark did the same.

Mark's arrival at Seattle Grace was epic. He definitely shook this place up. I mean, the man arrived in a towel! And, no, not one of those huge beach towels. It was more like a hand towel. Well, maybe not that small, but whatever towel he wore when he came out of Addison's shower was not big enough to cover the many rippling, bulging muscles that make up the sheer powerhouse of beef known as McSteamy. Catch my drift?

Okay, so I never directly saw this towel scene with my own two eyes. But, it's been described to me—in detail—several times. When Derek went over to Addison's hotel room one evening, he was mighty surprised to see McSteamy come out of the shower wearing that towel and nothing else. Derek was shocked, to say the least. He was even more shocked when he discovered that Mark was in fact moving to Seattle.

That was certainly an interesting time for the two former best buddies. Derek despised Mark. Rightfully so, I say. How could Derek have any trust left for his former best friend? Derek avoided Mark like the plague. They were no longer friends. As a matter of fact, Mark had been replaced. Oh, yes, Derek had made a new best friend at work. His name was Burke.

Derek and Burke started off as competition. Both of them wanted the Chief's job. You know, that's another common form of friendship here—making friends with the competition. It's also known as "frenemies." That's when you're friends with someone, but not really. You're fake friends. You're half-friends. You're just waiting for a chance to stab your frenemy in the back and take over the Chief of Surgery job that you deserve.

Personally, I don't recommend becoming a frenemy to anyone. "Frenemy" is a negative term. And, we don't like negative anything, remember? That's Principle Two! And we've already mastered that. It's all about the positive. Still, just be wary of these kinds of friends. It'd be quite unfortunate for you to get caught up with one.

Eventually, Derek and Burke graduated from frenemy to true friend. They went camping together, they'd go drinking together—Burke even asked Derek to be his best man. And he agreed! Friendship really is a beautiful thing, you know. And then, Burke *left*. So sad . . .

There will be more on Burke's story later, but Burke's exit left Derek without a best friend. He had no one to go camping with anymore. No one to grab a drink with, no one to talk to about his problems with Meredith—Derek had *no one*. And then, Mark stepped up to the plate again. It seemed that Derek really needed a friend as his relationship with Meredith was really being tested during that time. So, with Burke gone, Derek started confiding in Mark about Meredith. Hey, a good friend is cheaper than therapy, right?

I guess it's true what they say: Time heals all wounds. Because Derek and Mark were able to repair their friendship. It wasn't easy, but Derek forgave Mark for his previous transgressions. Today, Derek and Mark work together every day, side by side, joking around and enjoying their lives the way best friends should.

For a friendship to go through so much turmoil, it must've been pretty strong from the beginning. Derek and Mark's relationship was thoroughly tested, that's for sure. I, for one, don't know many men who can move on after such a blatant display of disrespect and mistrust by a friend. Apparently, however, Derek can. That's part of the reason he's known as McDreamy. He has many friends and is a friend to many people. Now, there's a man who values friendship. He appreciates the people in his life on a daily basis. Take note. Derek is a shining example of how to be a good friend. It's my hope that you can learn from his story and appreciate the good in people in your own life, too.

Okay, let me break it down for you: If you want to heal with love, you need to appreciate appreciation. You need to decide to be grateful. You need to choose to count your blessings. And you need to begin with your friendships. Because, as you can see, true friends are extraordinarily beautiful blessings. They're with you through both the best and the worst of times. They help you survive. Other than yourself, the one person who can help you heal with love is your friend. Your buddy, your comrade, your ally, your *person*. So, thank your friends for being your friends. Acknowledge and *appreciate* your friends. *Love* your friends and you will be loved in return.

HERONISM

Write the following affirmations down on a piece of paper:

"I can't help but think positively."

"I can't help but say 'thank you.' "

"I can't help but count my blessings."
"I can't help but appreciate the good things in my life."
"I can't help but feel grateful!"

Now, on the other side of your paper, I want you to list *three* things you are grateful for. Yes—just *three*! Easy breezy, right? If you can think of more than three, then, excellent! But, no pressure, k?

Start each sentence with, "I am grateful for . . ." Your list can be serious or humorous. It can focus on big things or small things. Your list can be specific or it can be general. The choice is yours! Okay, here's *my* list:

I am grateful for beautiful nights for saving lives.
I am grateful for the nurses that help me every single day.
I am grateful for McSteamy in a towel.

See? You can do that! Go ahead, construct your list now.

Okay, for the next seven days, I want you to read your piece of paper aloud, *every morning*. Both sides, too! Keep it in your nightstand or tape it to your bathroom mirror—just be sure to read that paper aloud every single day for the next seven days. After that, I want you to add *one* more item to your "grateful for" list every week. Continue adding to your list for however long you'd like. Keep it up and—pretty soon—you'll find yourself appreciating everyone and everything in your life! Thoughts of gratitude will come second nature to you, too.

CHAPTER FOUR

Become a Cheerleader (of Love)

"Love one another and you will be happy.
It's as simple and difficult as that."

—MICHAEL LEUNIG,
philosopher

WELL, LOOK AT YOU! You're three-fifths of the way there. About 60 percent done. That's a passing grade (when based on a curve). So, don't stop now! You're on your way to getting a solid A in Sydney's class—about to become a bona fide expert in the art of healing with love. Just two more principles to go! Easy breezy! Hey, you know what this calls for, right? Pop Quiz Numero Dos!

Which of the following DOES NOT belong?

A. Moonlight, flowers and candy
B. Ice cream
C. Snacks
D. Making someone feel like a freakin' lady
E. Trout for breakfast

Careful, now. Choose wisely. Tick-tock, tick-tock . . . Okay . . . And . . . Pencils down!

The correct answer is: E.

Why? Because choices A through D all symbolize "good dating etiquette." If you chose correctly, a gold star goes to you! And, if you chose incorrectly, please go read the rest of this chapter in a corner of your room (or, if you're outside, I want ten pushups while chanting, "I will learn to heal with love!" the entire time).

Alright, then. Principle Four focuses on the time-honored tradition known as dating. Now, I view a date as an opportunity to spread some love. It's as simple as that. You're basking in the warm glow of candlelight—gazing across the table at a handsome suitor who's raising a champagne flute into the air. A toast? To what, you ask. He responds—"To you." To *me*? You graciously accept, meeting his glass with yours—they clink—and your eyes smile with all the love in the world. The evening continues—you talk, you laugh, you delight. Positive thoughts abound. Appreciation flourishes. Love overflows.

What I'm trying to say is: Love is infectious. And dating is my transmission method of choice. If love is my religion, then I am an Evangelical Lover. Okay, that sounds a little scary. I'll just call myself a true cheerleader of love . . . Give me an L-O-V-E and give it to me when I'm on a date!

Question: Why is spreading love so important? Answer: Because the more people love, the more people *win* at this game of life. I firmly believe that if you put love out into the world, it'll come right back to you—often in the form of Mr. or Ms. Right. It's the answer to all of your problems. It's what my entire life philosophy is based on!

Look, love is like good news. And what do we do with good news? We spread it! Tell me, who doesn't like to share a bit of good news? Even better, who doesn't like to *hear* a bit of good news? Love should be thought of in the same respect.

And—take it from me—the best time to share and hear about love is on a date.

Go ahead, practice Principle Four the next time you're on a date and see what happens. Cheer my "heal with love" principles on! Spread the good news! You can be subtle, remember. You don't have to lecture your date on the benefits of saying "buh-bye" to stinkin' thinkin' as soon as you sit down at the dinner table! At least wait until after the appetizer! I'm only kidding, geez!

Here's the thing: If you've been practicing the previous three principles, then you're probably attracting good, positive people in your life. And, if you're dating, then your dates are being selected from that same group of good, positive people. And, if *that's* the case, then the person who's sitting across the table from you in the warm glow of candlelight is going to be just as into the whole "love" philosophy as well! Your heart will start to flutter and your blood pressure will rise. Your eyes will start to sparkle and your cheeks will turn rosy. Pretty soon, your lips will start to pucker and you won't be able to *stop* spreading the love. *This*, my friends, is how love is spread. Note that it's not blatant or abrasive. You're not shoving your newfound philosophy down your date's throat. Of course not! You're just doing something you can't help. You're a cheerleader of love. It's casual, subtle and sweet . . .

So, by all means, let your date hear your "heal with love" cheer! If, like you, your date is open and receptive to new ideas (and he/she *will be*), then why not talk about Principle One? Or, even Principle Three? Or, both?! What have you got to lose?

You'll soon realize that dating can be magical—*if* you do it right. That means no trout for breakfast, gentlemen. Nobody wants to eat trout for breakfast except *you*. It's just not sexy!

Last time I checked, dating was a two-player game. So, be considerate of your partner and refrain from putting a smelly fish on the table every morning. How about a nice breakfast soufflé? Or a tantalizing fruit spread? Even a quick and easy omelet is better than trout (just hold the cheese for me, please). But I digress.

Principle Four will be a natural progression in your heal with love transformation. As you continue on this journey, you'll want to tell others all about the healing power of love. And, as you master these principles—when you get really good at it—you'll want to spread the word as well. You'll find yourself telling *all* of your dates about it! That's when you know you've almost got that A in Sydney's favorite class: healing with love 101.

I should mention—if you're already in a committed relationship, being a cheerleader of love applies to you lucky souls, too! But, you probably already knew that! You probably tell your partner you love him/her on a daily basis. You do, don't you? Okay, good!

Wow, I'm telling you, those words: "I love you." Can't you just feel their weight and power? That sentence is the best kind of cheer. It's like a full-twist cradle/toe touch combo from a multi-level pyramid. Truly awesome. And, when you perform the actions that back those powerful words up? Well, then you're the epitome of love's biggest cheerleader. And you make Dr. Sydney Heron *very* proud.

Of course, not all of us have found our soul mates. But, until we do, we need to continue to spread the love. Continue to date. Continue to get into relationships. Speaking of which, allow me to tell you about a recent tryst of my own. It was a quick yet torrid affair. One in which I learned a great deal. The wounds, they're fully healed now—so please—read on . . .

My Ex-McDreamy: A Memoir

When you hear the words "morbidity and mortality," what's the first thing that pops into your mind? Death? Darkness? A fingernail puncturing a surgical glove making a woman's heart stop? Whatever it is, it's probably something negative, right? Wrong! People! You said buh-bye to those thoughts two principles ago. Get it together! Okay, let me tell you what *I* think of when I hear those words, "morbidity and mortality." It's positive . . . It's real . . . It's . . . handsome. It's . . . "McDreamy." Alright, here's the sitch!

Morbidity & Mortality conferences (also known as M & M's) are basically peer reviews of mistakes that have happened during the care of patients. M & M's occur every now and then at Seattle Grace. And, let me tell you, these things aren't exactly akin to big, exciting football games or your favorite band's sold-out concerts. Usually, M & M's are quite the opposite. Some austere hospital administrator lectures an auditorium full of doctors, and singles out the specific ones who have made errors when treating patients and it's all usually very serious and it's all usually very . . . *doom and gloom*. In short, M & M's are not the best way to spend an afternoon. *Usually.*

Now, I write (and italicize) *usually* because one particular M & M was *very* different for me. Instead of being all about doom and gloom, I remember this specific conference being all about good hair and the masculine scent of bergamot with a hint of pine. This wasn't your mother's M & M, okay?! Why? Because McDreamy was sitting right next to me.

Oh yes—At this particular M & M, I was clearly not paying attention to the negligent doctor pleading his case about Patient #29128. How could I? My elbow was touching the elbow of

Seattle Grace's most handsome, most capable, most divine brain surgeon. His hair so wavy and perfect. That smell so reminiscent of holidays spent in log cabins and chopped wood necessary to keep a cozy fire burning all . . . night . . . long . . . I remember this particular M & M like it was yesterday.

This was the closest I had ever gotten to McDreamy. Although, I knew all about him. *Every* woman at Seattle Grace knew all about him. For example, I knew McDreamy had moved to Seattle from Manhattan. He had a "thing" for ferry boats. Lived in a trailer in the woods (hence the scent). Liked to fly fish and eat muesli for breakfast. Had four sisters, nine nieces and five nephews. Oh, and if one were to look closely, one would notice a scar on his forehead. Some say this is from a motorcycle accident. Others maintain it's from the time he fought off a wild bear who got a little too close to his lady friend. And, still, some argue that McDreamy's scar is a result of rescuing a stray puppy from the side of a road back in New York. The puppy got a little too excited and nicked McDreamy's forehead. A small price to pay for giving a helpless animal another shot at life. Anyway, nobody knows for sure. My bet is on the wild bear story.

Of course, I also knew all about McDreamy dating his intern, Meredith. Which is why I kept my list of "Little Known Facts About McDreamy" to myself. Even when he asked if I had an extra pen, I simply shook my head "no" and smiled. McDreamy was taken. And, at that moment in time, I wasn't about to turn on my charm and steal him away from his intern. Sydney Heron may be many things, but a home wrecker she is not!

Now, I'm not crazy, I *do* realize that the events of that historic M & M *do not* constitute an official introduction between me and McDreamy. The details of that day remain fresh in my memory (I'm smelling that exquisite scent at this very moment), but I am *not* delusional. It was more of a brief encounter.

A quick meeting of the minds. A casual first acquaintance. Moreover, it was foreshadowing of good things to come . . .

Weeks passed. I had started to hear rumblings of a Mer-Der breakup. (Mer-Der, by the way, is the manner by which many doctors here at SGH refer to Meredith and Derek.) However, I dismissed the rumors as pure hearsay. One can *never* trust the rumors that fly around this place just about every day. But, when McSteamy took me aside and told me that Meredith and Derek had indeed split up—I must say—a wave of excitement came over me.

I realized that McSteamy wasn't exactly the most trustworthy source of information. That one's got a lot of tricks up his sleeve, I'm telling you! So, I decided to take charge of my destiny and go straight to the main man himself. I waltzed right up to Mc-Dreamy and *officially* introduced myself, yes I did. Oh, he was very receptive. A true gentleman. Which made me believe that—yes!—the Mer-Der breakup had officially occurred.

Throughout that day, McDreamy and I were absolutely lost in conversation after conversation. I remember one in particular—it was all about genealogy. I'm really into that sort of thing. I believe that you have to know where you come from in order to know where you're going. Well, as it turns out, Derek shared my interest in the subject! Yes—there are actual shepherds in his lineage. Fascinating, isn't it? Well, it didn't surprise me. He lives in a trailer. He chops wood. He catches trout. Here's a man who holds nature very near and dear to his heart. A man of his land. *Of course* McDreamy comes from a family of shepherds.

Our relationship blossomed soon after our official intro. I guess Derek just couldn't get me out of his head, because he asked me to Joe's. That's the bar across the street where *many* relationships have been born. It was going to be our first date. Our big announcement. We were about to become an official item and people were about to find out . . .

Now that Meredith was out of the picture, I allowed myself to open up to him that night at Joe's. The man intrigued me. It wasn't just his McDreamy smile or his McDreamy hair. It was his brain. His sense of humor. The way he operated, and not just in the OR. Oh, get your mind out of the gutter. What did I tell you about one night stands? Our stimulating conversation touched on everything from biology to goldfish to the origin of dry-erase boards. It was enthralling. I was, for sure, spreading the love. And, as far as I can tell, Derek was enjoying it. An hour later, we parted ways and I rushed home to work on this very book. I was happy. Truly content about my newfound relationship.

The following day, the entire hospital was buzzing about my relationship with McDreamy. It was *so* high school. After I heard some nurses giggling about "Sydrek," I decided to track my boyfriend down and fill him in on the gossip surrounding us. Well, I was surprised, to say the least, when I found my new boyfriend sitting on a bench outside with the one and only Meredith Grey. And, yep, they were *holding hands*. I stood there, in the lobby, shocked at what I saw. What were they talking about? Were they back together? What did this mean? At that exact moment, I made a decision: I had to end it.

Derek and I were an item for about twenty-four hours. Maybe less. I took McDreamy to Joe's and let him down softly. He just wasn't ready to be in the kind of relationship that I was interested in. So we laughed at the same things. So we had a lot in common. So we complemented each other extremely well. But, were we soul mates? I think not . . .

You know, I really should've been aware of this going into the relationship . . . McDreamy is nicknamed "McDreamy" for a reason. *I* am a healer. *I* heal people. *I* fix people. And Mc-Dreamy? There's really not a whole lot to fix there. He's practically perfect, alright? It's true. It was just a matter of time before good hair-having, sweet-smelling McDreamy was going to get old and stale. So, I decided to get out of that relationship when I had a chance. I think I made the right decision. I *know* I made the right decision. His heart remains with Meredith. And I can't be mad at him for that.

I really am grateful and thankful for my time with Derek. I may have lost a future lover, but I *gained* a friend. I look at the whole situation from this point of view: With McDreamy, I *tripped* over love. So I was able to get right back up. You see, that's the beauty and joy of dating. When you go out on a date, you're really just testing the waters. You go from one date to the next, learning what you like and, of course, what you don't. In the process, you're actually discovering a whole lot about yourself. I, for example, learned that many men, such as McDreamy, just won't be able to handle me. It's a fact! I'm a whole lot of woman. Independent. Confident. Meticulous. Punctual. A breadwinner, more or less. See what I mean? Dating helps identify your strengths and your weaknesses. Moreover, dating offers you the necessary tools *to grow*. And if you're able to grow, then you're able to heal.

Eventually, you'll find someone and you won't just *trip*, but you'll *fall* deeply, madly and passionately in love. You'll find someone who challenges and stimulates you. Someone who can handle you. Someone who can help you grow and, in the process, help you heal. And, well, there certainly won't be any getting up or coming back after that! Good luck out there!

CHAPTER FIVE

When in Doubt, Just Hug It Out

*"Failure is only the opportunity to
begin again more intelligently."*

—HENRY FORD

THERE COMES A time in every intern's life when all of his skills, techniques and knowledge are placed under a big, scary microscope. Intern Test Day. A day that determines the course of an intern's *entire* medical career. You can either pass—and continue down the road of doctorhood—or you can fail—and spend another long, difficult, embarrassing year as an intern. Basically, Test Day is the most important day of an intern's life . . .

All of that studying, all of that build-up, all of that preparation—Talk about pressure! Your whole career is riding on one little test! You have your flash cards, your extra No. 2 pencils, your backup deodorant, your good-luck charms and, of course, those freshly baked chocolate chip cookies your resident prepared in an effort to keep you calm, cool and collected on the big day. That last part? True story! Okay, I'll fill you in . . .

The night before a recent Test Day, I stayed up until four in the morning baking dozens and dozens of cookies for my then-interns. You know, I just thought it was a neat little way to cheer my students up and get rid of the butterflies in their tummies.

Just something to say, "I care. I *appreciate* all of your hard work." Well, would ya just look at that—Principle Three was in effect! Anyway, I brought my treats into work on that Test Day and my interns *devoured* them! Dr. Bailey noticed what I did and she looked at me like I was crazy! But, then again, Dr. Bailey looks at *everybody* like they're crazy. (Personally, I think Dr. Bailey was just a little embarrassed about not having the foresight to make her own interns some yummy treats.) Anyhoo—I'm happy to say that *all* of my interns passed their exams!

It's a shame I can't say the same thing about Dr. Bailey's interns. Maybe it was the lack of cookies? I can't say for sure . . . But, sadly, *one* of her interns failed the biggest test of his life. George.

Yes, George had one heck of an intern year. He endured ridicule after he was nicknamed "007," survived syphilis, withstood an interesting haircut, lost his father, got married and, now, failed his intern test. Needless to say, on that fateful Test Day, George was a bit distracted.

I, for one, wasn't too surprised about George's test results. Based on my interactions with the fellow prior to that day, I could tell—something just wasn't right with George. I later came to discover that the sensitive intern was caught in the middle of a love triangle between his wife and his best friend. Don't worry, you'll get the details about all of that later, but for now, we're just focusing on George and his intern test.

Like I said, George's mind was clouded with many disturbing thoughts that Test Day. Perhaps George's situation could've been assuaged by a good dose of positive thinking. Indeed, maybe all of George's stinkin' thinkin' was what ruined his chances of graduating. Perhaps George wasn't appreciating enough good things in his life. Maybe he was turning his back on his friends and failing to acknowledge them. We may never know what it was for sure. The fact is: George failed.

However, as F. Scott Fitzgerald once said, "Never confuse a single defeat with a final defeat." Words to live by, my dear friends.

After failing his intern test, George contemplated leaving the program altogether. He was *this* close to transferring to another hospital to start anew. When you fail, you see, all of these feelings of self-doubt and worthlessness begin to take control of your mind. George felt as if he had failed so many times on so many levels. He felt unsure. Useless. Like a fraud. Like a *failure*. The thing was—George didn't understand that failure is an *event* and can be overcome.

George needed to realize that all of the negative emotions and doubts that came along with failing his intern test *did not* define him. George needed to recognize the fact that everyone makes mistakes. That's how you learn! George didn't have to transfer to another internship program because he didn't pass his intern test. George didn't need to feel like a failure. He didn't need to feel unsure or useless or like a fraud because he made a few mistakes. No way, Jose! There's only *one* thing that George needed to do—he needed to hug it out.

Allow me to introduce Principle Five as well as your new life slogan: "When in doubt, just hug it out."

It's very, very simple. When you make a mistake and your world is filling with self-doubt: Hug it out!

Newsflash! You *are* going to fail sometimes! Trust me, you'll always pass failure on the road to success. It's like a rest-stop with a really dirty, smelly restroom somewhere between Trenton and Manhattan on the Jersey turnpike. (Sorry, I've visited a friend of mine who lives in Jersey only once and the stench of one particular rest-stop is a memory that I'll never be able to forget.) Anyway, my point is: Life is *not* a pass-or-fail course. You're going to have your ups and your downs. You'll win and you'll lose. You'll succeed and—that's right—you'll fail. It's just the name of the game.

That being said, when you *do* fail, you can't beat yourself up. You can't fix your problems by transferring to another hospital. The only thing you can do is ride out the repercussions. And, sometimes, it's a *really* long ride, so—while you're waiting for it to pass—there's only one thing to do: Hug it out! It just makes the ride much easier.

In the end, George decided to stay at Seattle Grace. And, boy, it's a good thing he did! He would've been missed, let me tell you. I guess he realized that running from his problems wasn't the best solution. George needed to stick it out *and* he needed to hug it out. I'm glad that he made the right choice.

Almost anyone here at SGH will tell you, Sydney Heron practices what she preaches. Yes, when in doubt, I hug it out. Okay, okay, I can't help it! There's just something about hugging another person that makes all of your fears and worries *disappear*. Try it sometime and you'll see what I mean. But before you do that, I'd like to share another story with you. A story that brings all five principles of healing with love into play. A story that's all about making mistakes, being consumed with self-doubt and eventually needing to just hug it out . . .

A Cold? Nope, It's Spinal Fluid!

I have a friend who waitresses at one of those fancy schmancy restaurants downtown. I know—it's hard to imagine surgeons having friends *outside* of the hospital, but, we do! Anyway, Karen—that's my friend—has been in the service industry for years. She has days both good and bad. Karen decides which is which based on the amount of tips she receives throughout a particular day.

Obviously, the more tips, the better the day. After a "good" day, Karen is able to leave work with a smile on her face, confident. However, after a "bad" day, Karen leaves work dejected, morose, sad . . . She's upset and calls herself a "failure." She probably mixed up a certain customer's order. Or forgot to refill a drink. Or she wasn't fast enough. Whatever the case may be, Karen beats herself up and begins to analyze every single mistake she made during the course of that day. Then, she calls me—sometimes sobbing— *oftentimes* sobbing—and I make her feel all better.

I remind Karen about the power of healing with love. I tell her to meet me at the Pike Place Market where we proceed to hug it out. And, before I know it, Karen's nose has been wiped clean, her mascara has stopped running, her neck has stopped twitching and her face has returned to its normal color. (Karen, ladies and gentlemen, takes her job *very* seriously.)

After Karen leaves, I can't help but reflect on *my* job at the hospital as opposed to Karen's job at the steakhouse. When surgeons make a mistake, you see, somebody could end up *dead*. A customer doesn't receive his tuna tartare on time and wonders about his free diet soda refill? Easy breezy! Try misdiagnosing a patient. Try amputating the wrong foot. Try accidentally leaving a towel in a patient after an operation instead of accidentally leaving Table 12's food at Table 17. Yes—the stakes are certainly a little higher where *I* work.

I probably shouldn't tell you this, but do you know how often doctors make mistakes? Well, *pretty often*. While operating, our minds are filled with the same kind of worry, doubt and fear that plagues people like Karen while waitressing. But you didn't hear it from me, okay?

Just last year, a thirty-something patient came into the clinic. By the way, the clinic was something Bailey helped create in an attempt to gain recognition for the Chief Resident position.

Bailey will deny it, but *I* know it's true. More on that later . . .
Anyhoo! This guy comes into the clinic with a bright, red shiny
nose. It was Rudolph reincarnated as a man who had a severe
cold. At least, I *thought* it was a cold . . .

But, at that point, all I knew was that Rudolph was in the hospital because of a severe runny nose. He had just met a special
girl and certain "activities" were placed on hold between the couple because of Rudolph's sinus issues. Needless to say, the guy was
desperate to get better. He needed his nose to stop dripping all
over the place so he could seal the deal with his new lady friend.

I treated this particular patient with intern Izzie. Now, I was
used to seeing Izzie pay extra attention to her patients. She's really all about patient care, so I was completely taken aback when
Izzie tried to discharge Rudolph, saying that it was "just a cold."
No, no, no! That's where Izzie was wrong. This "cold" that Izzie
was speaking about was one of the greatest unsolved medical
mysteries of our time! As doctors, it was our *duty* to provide our
patient with some sort of relief. I ordered Izzie to perform a
nasal lavage on our dear, red-nosed, messy Rudolph. Izzie listened, because that's what interns do (usually).

I thought that day was going to be one of my good days. You
see, successfully treating patients is *my* version of Karen receiving lots of tips. I was in the clinic the whole day, providing
Grade A patient care to a number of patients. Throat cultures,
blood tests, immunizations, nasal lavages . . . That day was definitely going to be a good day! Or, so I thought (positively, I
might add) . . .

That night, however, I learned that Rudolph didn't really have
a cold at all. The patient actually had a hole in his dura. He was
leaking spinal fluid out of his nose. Had a brain herniation, a de-
fect that was there since his birth. And it was just waiting to
blow. My order for a nasal lavage was essentially useless. You see,

nasal lavage doesn't really do much when your spine is leaking out of your face. I was wasting this man's time. I failed to diagnose him more closely. I made a mistake. A *big* mistake.

Luckily, my error didn't cost this man his life. And, yes, he ended up sealing the deal with his lady friend. But, my mistake *could've* prevented that from happening . . .

After that day, I started to doubt myself and my abilities as a surgeon. I found myself working in constant fear that I was going to make *another* mistake—one that could cost a patient's life. I questioned myself. I doubted myself. I actually started to make excuses and come up with reasons why I was unable to scrub in! It was really bad . . .

So, you know what I did? You got it—I called up Karen, met her at Pike Place and . . . *hugged it out*. And, as I was standing there—smelling the fresh seafood along the pier, my arms wrapped around Karen in a giant bear hug, my eyes glassy—I made a decision. I decided to seize the day. I decided to stop thinking about Bailey and how impressed the Chief must be with her after the opening of the clinic. I realized that in and of itself was probably the reason why I misdiagnosed Rudolph. I was distracted. I was too concerned with Bailey and her shameless self-promotion. That was stinkin' thinkin' and I needed to say buh-bye to it! Yes, as I hugged Karen a little tighter—spreading the love and letting my friend know just how much I appreciated her—I began to heal myself. With love!

You see, the act of hugging allows you to consider and feel the very essence of love. You'll never find yourself mad when you're hugging someone. Very rarely will a negative thought flash through your mind as your arms are wrapped tightly around another person. Hugging provides a moment of sincere, honest human contact that enables your mind to ponder the idea of love. It's a chance to remember the principles of healing with love and it's an opportunity to decide to put those principles into effect.

The day after my extended hug-a-thon with Karen, I walked through the front doors of Seattle Grace with my head held high. I was *determined* to scrub in that day and prove to myself that I was anything but ordinary. Anything but a failure. Well, what do you know? I succeeded! Because I was able to turn my attitude around, scrub into an advanced procedure, kick some booty and save a life! That night, I even went on a date! That's right, to spread some love! Yes! Dr. Sydney Heron was back! Hugging it out *works*. You'll see . . .

This last principle of healing with love really sums up my entire philosophy. "When in doubt, just hug it out." Come on—say your new slogan loud and proud, friends! This is the culmination of *all* of my principles. Practicing Principles One through Four will make mastering Principle Five possible. *That's* how one is supposed to heal with love.

First, seize the day and decide to heal with love *now*, in the present moment. (And, remember, be careful about healing with *too much* love.) Second, say "hasta la vista" to any and all negative thoughts. Embrace the positive! Third, appreciate the good things in your life—starting with your friends. Thank them, appreciate them, *love* them. Fourth, become the power of love's biggest cheerleader. Spread love (safely) to as many people as you can. And, finally, because you can't avoid failure: When in Doubt, Just Hug It Out!

HERONISM

Still bothered by a mistake you made in the past? Well, then, *this* is the perfect exercise for you: Create your own stickers!

Go to any craft store and buy whatever catches your eye. Glitter, finger paint, little shiny butterfly cutouts. Stock your cart with whatever crafts your heart desires! You'll also need to stop by the grocery store and get some unflavored gelatin.

When you get home, design your stickers! Use the glitter, finger paint, little shiny butterfly cutouts and whatever else you picked up to create unique designs on paper. Cut them out in cute little designs. Write fun little words on them— "Super!" "Rock Star!" "Cardiogod!" Remember, your sticker can say whatever you'd like . . .

Now, put your stickers face down on a sheet of aluminum foil. In a small bowl, mix the unflavored gelatin with half a cup of warm water. Stir the mixture until the gelatin is fully dissolved. Then, using a paintbrush, brush the mixture onto the backs of your stickers. Let dry.

Your stickers are now ready to be licked! Moistening the backs of the stickers (the gelatin side) makes them "sticky." Feel free to place your stickers anywhere you'd like! On your forehead? On your walls? On your scrubs? It's all up to you! In addition to hugging it out, this exercise is a surefire way to feel a little better about previous mistakes! Beat the blues with homemade stickers! And—of course—have fun!

Now that you understand and have (hopefully) learned the five principles of healing with love, it's time to put them into action! Oh, this is where it gets good! Remember, you can heal *everything* with love. Let's begin with relationships . . .

PART TWO

Healing Relationships

with Love

CHAPTER SIX

Pick Me. Choose Me.
Love Me. And Mean It!

"Losers make promises they often break.
Winners make commitments they always keep."

—DENIS WAITLEY,
author and motivational speaker

OKAY, I'M JUST going to let the cat out of the bag here—
I am a doer. Guilty! You can ask any of my friends and
they'll confirm it's true. I mean, come on—becoming a surgeon,
dating McDreamy—those are no small feats. What can I say?
I'm a woman who knows what she wants and knows how to get
it. I act. I achieve. I commit. And believe me, as a surgeon, I can
tell you a thing or two about that last part: commitment.

It takes years of medical training, tons of hard work, one very
positive attitude and oodles of commitment to become a top
surgeon at Seattle Grace. You've got to be strong, intelligent and
determined. You've got to be thick-skinned. You've got to be re-
sourceful. If you want to make it around here, you *cannot* be
someone who gives up when the going gets tough. And, trust
me, times are going to get tough. You can't just run home and
bury your head in your pillow! You can't just run across the street,
order nine shots of tequila and go home with a sexy brain surgeon. That, my friends, is a *much different* kind of doer. One who
takes "loving in the present moment" a little too far. One who

shies away from our word of the day here: commitment. One who clearly needs a little help healing with love.

You may have guessed—I'm talking about Meredith Grey here. The Meredith who is actually a very talented and capable surgeon. The Meredith who had a world-renowned, famous surgeon as a mother. The Meredith who should clearly—*positively*— know a few things about commitment! Yet, for some reason, she does not. Why, Meredith? Why? Why do you freeze up every time your boyfriend mentions building a house with you? Why do you fight the urge to run in the opposite direction when your man brings up marriage? Why do you tremble at the thought of a lifetime in McDreamy's arms? Why?! Oh, Meredith, why do you hurt Sydney so?

Well, here's the short answer: Because Meredith doesn't know how to heal with love. Sadly, Meredith thinks it's better to break her word than do worse by keeping it. And I'm shaking my head. I'm pursing my lips. I'm thinking to myself, "Meredith has *a lot* to learn, *a lot* to change and *a lot* of fears to overcome." She's wounded, that one. Like a tiny, abandoned kitten. Well, I've got some advice for her. Meredith, for one, needs to lick her wounds clean with the power of love. Oh, what's that? She doesn't know *how*? *You* don't know how? Well, it's *never* too late to learn . . .

From what I've seen and heard with my very own eyes and ears, Meredith has an intrinsic fear of commitment. (You could be dealing with this very same issue, which is why you're reading this very closely. Am I right?) Now, I could easily trace this fear of Meredith's (and yours) back to childhood. Back to overbearing parents. But, let's save all of that for later. Instead, I'm going to trace Meredith's fear of commitment—with McDreamy, specifically—back to the arrival of a certain red-haired, salmon-scrub-wearing, world-renowned, neonatal surgeon . . . better known as Addison—Derek's wife.

When Addison showed up—clad all in black, how *very* New York—a serious wrench was thrown into SGH's most infamous relationship between attending and intern. Derek, naturally, was quite surprised by his wife's abrupt arrival. And Meredith, as you can imagine, was devastated.

At that point, Meredith did what any woman would do in the same situation: She evaluated her boyfriend's leggy and fabulous wife. And, well, Mer felt like she paled in comparison. Here's Meredith—a lowly first-year intern who's lucky to scrub in on a basic procedure. And, there's Addison—a distinguished surgeon who practices cutting-edge medicine just about every day. Yes—Addison was clearly both a force of nature and a major blow to Meredith's ego.

On top of all that—Meredith soon discovered that Derek hadn't yet signed his divorce papers. It seemed that Derek was having some doubts of his own. He wasn't sure he wanted to sign on the dotted line and end his eleven-year marriage. That's eleven Thanksgivings, eleven birthdays, eleven Christmases. And Derek was supposed to sign a piece of paper to end his family? It wasn't an easy decision. So, in the end, Derek decided to stay with his wife.

Let me just say this: Ladies, if you're ever unfortunate enough to come face to face with your boyfriend's previously unmentioned wife, *do not*—and I repeat, *do not*—mosey on over to your nearest pub and drown your sorrows in tequila. That's what Meredith did. And it didn't help her one bit! When Derek decided to pick, choose and love Addison, Meredith thought she needed liquor—*fast*. However, what Meredith *really* needed was a hug! But, what's the one thing we know about Meredith? That's right—she doesn't know how to heal with love.

Now, obviously, the ordeal known as Addisongate wounded Meredith's soul. A deep wound. The kind that'll rip stitches wide open. Still, alcohol is *not* the best course of treatment. Thinking positively—sure. Calling up a girlfriend for a quick gab fest—why not? Hugging it out—well, you can't go wrong with that one! The only thing liquor is good for is a hangover. After Meredith sobered up, she was *still* the girl who didn't get picked.

I saw Meredith the night she didn't get picked. Drunk as a skunk, I'm telling you! The poor thing was walking around the hospital with a banana bag attached to her arm. There was a massive train wreck and bodies were pouring into the ER. I'll never forget seeing one couple impaled together on a single pole! It was quite a sight, a real whirlwind of activity. And there was Meredith, unable to practice medicine because she had a big ol' sloppy hangover. It was just Mer and her banana bag. You see, when you pour tequila on a wound, it *stings*. And, believe me, Meredith was definitely feeling the sting at that particular moment in time.

The period that followed was a trying time for Meredith. She had to stand by and watch Derek attempt to make his marriage with Addison work. She fell under harsh, critical scrutiny from her peers. She had to work with her ex-boyfriend's wife practically every day. I remember, one time, seeing a perfect coifed Addison standing near a "Hello, Kitty" bandaged Meredith. Oh, it must've been awful for Meredith. All of the awkward elevator moments, the hair-smelling, the ensuing one night stands, the *many more ensuing* one night stands . . . Oh, Meredith . . .

Oh, yes, there was one story in particular that I remember hearing about very vividly. If my sources are correct, then his name was Steve Murphy. Meredith met him at, where else, Joe's. Well, the day after their romp, Steve showed up at the hospital with a case of priapism. That is, Steve had a neurological problem that caused his erection to last forever! And, you know what neurological calls for: McDreamy! That's right, Derek had to operate on Meredith's one night stand. An awkward day for everyone. And another reason why you should never go to a bar, drink your problems away and take someone home . . . They might just show up at your workplace the next day with Captain Winkie at a permanent full salute—know what I mean?

Anyway, where was I? That's right, after all was said and done . . . After Addison robbed Meredith of her McDreamy, her McDog and her McLife . . . after the bomb in the body cavity, after sex with George (don't ask), after a fling with a local veterinarian, after all the knitting . . . Meredith's rocky relationship with Derek culminated in secret closet sex at the Prom.

Lesson To Be Learned #9,134: *Do not* have secret closet sex at the Prom with your ex-boyfriend who is married.

Lesson To Be Learned #9,135: *Do not* lose your panties while having secret closet sex at the Prom with your ex-boyfriend who is married!

Yes, Derek "accidentally" left Meredith's panties in his tuxedo jacket after having secret closet sex with Meredith. I put "accidentally" in quotes because nobody knows if Derek's error was an accident or an "accident." Two *very* different things.

At any rate, Addison found the panties the very next day. And that, my students, was the end of Derek and Addison's marriage. Hey, they gave it a shot, but it just didn't work. Why? Because Meredith and Derek are *soul mates.* They belong together. Therefore, anything that comes in between them will be *destroyed.* At least, I believe so. That's how it's *supposed* to work. That's how the fairy tale is *supposed* to end . . . *If* only Meredith could get over this deep-rooted fear of commitment and learn to heal with love!

Alas, as you can see, that's a big *if.* Meredith *thinks* she has several reasons to be scared of devoting her life to McDreamy. That's just it—Meredith *thinks* so. She *chooses* to think so. And,

as we all know, she can *choose* to either think positively or negatively (the good vs. the bad; the ponies vs. the pink mist).
Meredith—and only Meredith—can decide her destiny. So,
what's it gonna be, Mer?

Meredith won't just come out and answer that question on
the spot. No, Meredith is going to be hesitant because, well,
Meredith is Meredith. She's still an *intern* at heart. She's the
Ten-Year-Old, new at this whole relationship thing. Meredith
doesn't know what to do after seeing her best friend get jilted at
the altar (more to come, don't worry). She doesn't realize that a
prolonged bout of breakup sex does more harm than good. She
doesn't know how to react when her boyfriend presents her with
blueprints of their dream home and admits to kissing a surgical
scrub nurse named Rose (yes, I'll get to *that*, too).

But, here's the thing: Meredith isn't *supposed* to know how to
deal with any of that. She's learning, just like you. And, when
you allow yourself to learn—when you allow yourself to overcome your fears and correct your mistakes—you're healing with
love.

So, if *you* are dating a McDreamy . . . If *you*—for some
reason—feel inadequate standing next to him . . . try imple-
menting those five principles you just learned in part one. When
your McDreamy unveils his plans for your dream home, for example, then:

- *Do not* immediately go to any of the following thoughts:
  being choked, smothered, controlled or overwhelmed.
- *Do not* buy into the whole idea of losing one's sense of self.
- *Do not* become frightened by the thought of going to bed
  with and waking up next to the same person for the rest
  of your life.
- *Do* think positively.

· *Do* find a friend.

· *Do* hug it out.

Come on—you can do it. Why? Because it's a choice! *Choose* to think positively. Moving in with a boyfriend is something to look forward to! Living with the person you love, your soul mate? That's not a threat! And, if you *still* think it is, then you're not ready. So, be honest with your mate and tell him. *Communicate*. If he really is your soul mate, then he'll understand.

It's true—learning and overcoming your fears (whether they're commitment-based or not) *isn't* an easy process. For Meredith, and for any Merediths reading this right now, *stop* going to bars. *Stop* getting drunk. *Stop* sleeping with inappropriate men. You may be thinking, "But Sydney, that's easier said than done!" Nonsense, I say! You need to make a decision right now, in the present moment, to love yourself and *change*. It goes back to the very first principle. To change one's life, start immediately. Do it flamboyantly! Call up your best friend for a little chitchat. Spread some love. Hug it out. Just do anything except go to that bar and order tequila. Trust in Sydney and you'll eventually discover that healing with love isn't as hard as Meredith makes it look.

HERONISM

Let's get you on the road to overcoming your fears! Did you know that you have the power to squash every last one of them? Well, you do! Your fear of commitment, your fear of abandonment, your fear of your boyfriend's leggy and fabulous wife . . . you can beat 'em all!

First, you need to *identify* your fears. List them on a piece of paper. Number them—one through however many fears you have . . . Then, for each fear, answer the following question: How do you know you're afraid? What's the *reason*? Write your response next to that particular fear. So, for example, let's say you listed "Commitment" as Fear #1. If you then asked yourself "how you know you're afraid," then you might write, "Because I fight the urge to run in the opposite direction every time my boyfriend says he's in love with me." Continue this process for each and every fear on your list.

Next, lie down on your bed—with your paper—and begin to read your fears (and their reasons) aloud. Start each sentence with, "I am afraid of <fear> because <reason>." Say them slowly. Remain calm. Remember to breathe.

When you're finished, close your eyes and think about what you just said. Notice that you were able to read your fears and reasons without losing control? Congratulations! You just identified your fears and didn't let them get the best of you! You didn't run in the opposite direction. You didn't kick McDreamy out of your bed. You *remained in control*. And that was the point of this exercise.

Repeat this Heronism *at least* once a week. Sooner or later, your fear-based issues will vanish. You'll actually start to become more comfortable with your fears. Eventually, when your boyfriend says he's in love with you, you won't fight the urge to run the other way. Instead, you'll actually stand there and listen. And, maybe—just maybe—you'll say, "I love you, too."

CHAPTER SEVEN

Nobody's Perfect.
Not Even You, Mr. Shaky Hands.

"Have no fear of perfection—
you'll never reach it."

—SALVADOR DALÍ

So you're not perfect. That's not exactly a shock, right? I mean, you're human. And humans make mistakes—it's what we do. It's how we learn. It's why pencils have erasers. Of course, some mistakes are worse than others. For example, accidentally crashing into a supply cart as you hurriedly round a corner? Embarrassing, but not inexcusable. Misreading the handwriting on a patient chart and telling a patient she's dying when she's really not? Okay, that one's really bad. Oh, deciding to operate on a patient when you have a hand tremor? That's even worse! The point is, whether we're just clumsy, tired or one of the nation's leading cardiothoracic surgeons afraid of what the future may hold, *all of us* make mistakes.

You know who I really feel sorry for? Baseball players. Sure, they look like they're having tons o' fun out there—making *a lot* of money just for playing a silly little game in the middle of a field. The fancy cars, the big homes, the trophy wives . . . On the surface, being a professional athlete seems like it'd be kind of great, right? But, when you think about it, those baseball players have their errors counted and published every single day of their lives! Now, imagine that! The public scrutiny, the constant ridicule, the harsh spotlight on all of your mistakes . . . Those boys sure pay a hefty price for living the high life.

No, the rest of us don't have to endure a daily tally of our errors—so, be grateful for that! We can misdiagnose leaking spinal fluid for a runny nose, learn from the situation, and put it behind us. We can place our hands on a bomb in a body cavity, pledge to *never*, *ever* do such a thing again, and move on. We can keep quiet about our boyfriend's hand tremor, have the whole thing blow up in our face, then forgive and ultimately forget. The only *real* mistake that exists is when a person learns nothing after making one. So, embrace your mistakes! The next time you make one, when you're with your *person*—hugging it out—I want you to think about what you can learn from the situation. And, trust me, there *will* be a next time. Like I said, you're human. You're not a robot. Right?

. . . Right?

You look unsure. Come on, talk about your feelings. It's important to dialogue. Alright, I know what this calls for! Pop quiz! Here's a little quiz to determine whether you do, in fact, sometimes, kinda-sorta, act a little bit like . . . *a robot*.

Answer the following questions with either a simple YES or a NO:

A. Is your favorite color red, like blood?
B. Have you ever needed to be sedated because of your mother's presence?
C. Do you think nurses and/or psych interns are inferior human beings?

D. If you were a teacher, would you ever refer to your students by numbers?

E. Prior to reading this book, did the thought of "talking about your feelings" send chills down your spine?

F. Does it still?

Pencils down! Alright, if you answered "yes" to *any* of the above statements, then—I'm sorry—you *do* exhibit some signs of being a robot. And, if you answered "yes" to *all* of the above statements, then you, my dear, *go to jail!* Do not pass Go! Do not collect $200! Sit there, in your cell, and read this book again. This time, *pay attention!*

Of course, if you answered "no" to all of those statements, then congratulations! Pat yourself on the back and give yourself a hug. Here's to you! You're keeping up! You're in the lead! Healing with love, here you come!

(Okay, so maybe I was a little harsh on the robots. But, what do they care? They're *robots*. They don't have feelings. Fine. I'm all about second chances, so . . . Robots? You can continue reading, it's okay. This chapter is especially for all of *you*, anyway.)

Whereas humans will make mistakes and learn from them, robots don't know what to do when they realize they're not perfect. Humans can misjudge, miscalculate, misdiagnose—and they will *accept* the fact that they're flawed. Robots, on the other hand, will be all "malfunction, malfunction" and "I will self-destruct in 30 seconds." I just did my "robot" voice. Too bad you couldn't hear it. Anyway, the fact that you're continuing to read this book tells me that you're not all R2-D2. You care enough about yourself—and the people around you—to give this whole healing with love thing a shot. You want to dialogue. You want to love. You want to feel. I think that's splendid! So kudos to you!

I so desperately want one particular doctor around here to read this book. In fact, when it's published, I just might stick a complimentary copy in her cubby. A little present, a little surprise. It's really the least I could do. This doctor's name? Cristina. Her diagnosis? A severe case of robotitis. Her cure? This book, silly!

Now, Cristina is definitely a doctor who strives for perfection. That's putting it rather mildly! It's sad, really. Striving for perfection is dangerous because it's unattainable, you know. Her ex-boyfriend, the shaky-hand cardio surgeon I previously mentioned—Dr. Burke—well, he's not much different. Unfortunately, both of them chose to go after perfection instead of excellence. And, that's exactly how they got into trouble. Intrigued? Well, then keep on reading!

I first met Cristina when I subbed for her regular resident, Dr. Bailey. As a matter of fact, that's when I first met *most* of the people I'm telling you about in this book. What can I say— they're a memorable bunch! Anyway, Dr. Bailey had a little bun in the oven, so she was put on bed rest. Strict orders! So, I was chosen to take care of Bailey's interns. Yes, it was I, Sydney Heron, reporting for duty!

Cristina was the first one of the wild bunch I officially met. I remember seeing her, standing there, staring at me rather blankly. Cristina looked like she needed a friend. So, I did what I normally do—I enveloped her in one great, big, fuzzy hug. I held her close, smiling. And, well, do you know what she said to me at that moment in time?

Cristina had the nerve to mutter, "Ow." Yes—"Ow." I thought I was hurting her. But, no, that wasn't it. I was *touching* her. And, well, Cristina didn't like to be touched.

From that moment on, Cristina's robot qualities became more and more noticeable to me. She made fun of her peer, George, for standing behind the nurses' strike line like a—oh, what was it—oh, yes, "a little girl." The nurses, if I recall correctly, were on strike during that time. George was standing up for what he believed in. He was a union man! He was *my* kind of man, let me tell you!

Cristina also showed very little sympathy for a woman who came into the hospital that day. The woman, Claire, was on an "adventure" honeymoon with her husband when she discovered a nasty looking rash on her leg. Actually, they had just been hiking on Mt. Rainier. Well, we inspected Claire's wound and soon discovered that the rash was not just any old rash. It was necrotizing fasciitis. More commonly known as flesh-eating bacteria.

Oh, that poor girl. It had already spread over most of her leg. Cristina and I had to break the news to Claire's husband. I, for one, hate giving bad news. It's like I'm forced to spread negativity when I have to inform loved ones and patients of their scary fate. Cristina, on the other hand, seemed a little odd—almost excited about the prospect of Claire's pending surgery. According to Cristina, amputating Claire's foot was the only sane option at that point. But, I promised Claire's husband that I would do everything in my power to save Claire's leg.

I remember seeing very little compassion from Cristina while working with her on Claire's case. Cristina wanted to cut. That's all she cared about. It seemed like Cristina had a one-track mind. Cutting off a woman's leg—now *that* would be a cool surgery. Indeed, an amputation would be an interesting learning experience for Cristina. But, did she realize that, by doing so, we would in effect be taking away our patient's identity? Claire wasn't 80. She was 25! She wasn't unhealthy. She and her husband signed up for an "adventure" honeymoon! Yes, it seemed like "adventure" was Claire's middle name! And now Cristina wanted to cut off this woman's leg, ensuring that our patient will never be able to hike or climb or take part in another "adventure" for the rest of her life? Where was Cristina's consideration? Where were Cristina's feelings?

During Claire's surgery, I remained strong. I promised I would save her leg and—gosh darn it—I was *going* to save her leg. I wasn't going to let Cristina's criticism of my doctoring skills get to me. Moreover, I wasn't going to let Dr. Burke get to me . . .

Oh yes—Cristina called Dr. Burke in to "check up on me" during Claire's surgery. I had never met Dr. Burke prior to that. I just knew him from his exquisite reputation as one of the nation's top cardio surgeons. But, the moment Burke came into my OR, I *knew* . . .

Cardio surgeons don't see too many cases of flesh-eating bacteria, you know. It's a little out of their jurisdiction. So, Burke was just there because Dr. Yang was concerned about my medical judgment. I was insulted, but I kept my eyes on the prize. That is, I remained focused on saving Claire's leg. Despite Cristina's unkindness and lack of compassion, I ended up saving my patient's leg. Yes, I ended up saving my patient's life.

I later discovered that Burke and Cristina were, in fact, a couple. I wasn't surprised, really. Keeping Burke's excellent reputation in mind, I knew there had to be something more to the story. The Burke that I read and heard about wouldn't just waltz into another surgeon's OR and question her medical skills. No, there was something *else* pushing him to do such a tacky thing. That something else was his relationship with an intern.

Dr. Burke and Cristina—what a pair, those two. They sure had *a lot* in common. Independent and strong-willed. Extremely ambitious. Interested in all things cardio. Not exactly verbose. And, of course, they were perfectionists. They were always striving for perfection, never knowing how to deal whenever (and if ever) they fell short.

Even though Burke is no longer a doctor at Seattle Grace, he's still talked about and remembered very vividly to this day. Burke was a surgeon used to being the best in his field. He was very, very good. He was at the pinnacle of his career, vying for the Chief of Surgery position at SGH. Some even said that Burke had the job in the bag. And then, the unthinkable happened. He suffered a gunshot wound to his right shoulder and his career was put on hold . . .

Burke was badly injured. The gunshot having caused a slight tremor in Burke's hand, his entire career was in jeopardy. Would he ever be able to operate again? Certainly not with that hand tremor! It was an imperfection. And Burke didn't know how to deal with it. He became listless and depressed. I mean, Burke was used to being at the top of his game—perfectly confident, perfectly operating, simply *perfect*—until now.

It took him quite a while to recover from his imperfection— both physically and mentally. But, after a lot of practice and a lot of positive thinking, Burke eventually got himself back to his previous level. He said he was "fine." So Derek cleared him for surgery and Burke began operating once again. Naturally, Cristina was extremely happy. She got her mentor and teacher back. Remember what I said earlier? Cristina and Burke, they were quite the team. However, both of them, at that point, were hiding a deep, dark secret.

You see, Burke was *not* fine. Unbeknownst to Derek and the rest of the hospital, Burke's tremor persisted. And the only two people who knew about it? Cristina and Burke. For a time, Cristina was covering for and hiding Burke's secret imperfection. During their surgeries, Cristina and Burke thought they made the *perfect* team. For every maneuver Burke couldn't complete because of his shaky hand, Cristina sprang into action, and vice versa. The *perfect* machine. The *perfect* robot. Just . . . *perfect*.

But, as we all know, perfection is unattainable. So, Cristina and Burke's secret was bound to get out.

It was actually Cristina who first went to the Chief and told him the truth. Oh, what a day that was! The Chief ultimately decided not to punish Cristina and Burke for their actions—he was only interested in getting Burke better. Eventually, Derek re-operated on Burke's shoulder, fixing the hand tremor once and for all. Still, both Burke and Cristina (and, some would argue, this hospital) were never the same.

Yes, Cristina and Burke discovered that perfection is impossible. And they discovered it the hard way. Sadly, like so many of us, I'm sure they continue to wrestle with thoughts of imperfection every single day. The thing is, instead of aiming for perfection, all of us need to aim for *excellence*.

As long as I'm trying my hardest, being excellent at something is good enough for me. And it should be for you, too. Remember that the next time you mess something up or your hand starts to shake. Hey, it's going to happen! You're a *person*. You're not a robot, remember? Human nature tells us that we're all going to make mistakes. So recognize them. Accept them. Embrace them. Most importantly, *love* them! And in doing so, you'll be able to learn from your past and ultimately heal. Your blunders, you see, are a lot like building blocks. They provide the structure of our characters. They help us remain strong. They allow us to make better decisions in the future. Utilizing them allows each and every one of us to grow into bigger, better, healthier human beings.

CHAPTER EIGHT

Honesty and You

*"If you tell the truth you don't have
to remember anything."*

—MARK TWAIN

LET'S SAY YOU'RE IN the middle of some really great dream. Maybe happy little munchkins are singing "Happy Birthday" to you or the Chief is congratulating you on your recent promotion to Chief Resident or perhaps you're even reliving the time you were named Homecoming Queen and Valerie Kapinski is staring at you, fuming, with that wretched look of disgust on her face. *Whatever* the case may be, you're in dreamland. You're at peace, enjoying a restful slumber. And, well, Valerie Kapinski just made you stir a little bit, so what do you do? You roll over and reach out for your McDreamy who's sleeping right next to you. Just a little snuggle, a little cuddle. The thing is, though, when you open your eyes to look at your sleeping McDreamy, you realize he's not sleeping at all. In fact, he's staring right at you. *Watching* you sleep. Which is kinda creepy, right? Maybe even more creepy than Valerie Kapinski. But, then your McDreamy smiles and nods and sighs and you fall right back asleep, returning to dreamland. At peace again, enjoying a restful slumber . . .

Until the very next night, when it happens again.

You know, that whole McDreamy-watching-you-sleep thing. He's *still* watching you sleep. And it's *still* creepy. But, you know—deep in your heart—that McDreamy can't really be creepy. It's impossible, by definition. So, then, if he's not watching you sleep, what is he really doing? *That's* when the truth comes out. Your McDreamy can't sleep. Why? Because *you* snore. Oh, the horror!

Even though you're embarrassed . . . Even though you're slightly ashamed . . . Even though you're beginning to accept that, yes, you have flaws . . . Take pleasure in the fact that your boyfriend did a very noble, responsible thing: He told the *truth*. And, my friends, telling the truth is one of the most important things you can do for your relationship. When it comes to healing with love, honesty is the best policy because, well, truth is love and love is truth. Just go with me, people.

If the scenario described above should ever happen to you, try to not take it personally. Just because someone told you the truth and pointed out your breathing imperfection, it's *not* okay to start pointing out that person's flaws in retaliation. It may be your first instinct to accuse that person of having bad breath or tell that person it's impossible to kiss him because he hasn't shaven in days, but *try* to refrain! Yes, you could be telling the truth, too, but I'm afraid you're being brutally honest . . . for the sake of just being brutal. It's important to dialogue, but skip all of the personal attacks. They don't get you anywhere. It just leads to more and more fighting. And, what fun is that, really? You're focusing on the negative when there's a very clear positive that needs to be encouraged and addressed here: Your partner isn't a liar!

Trust is the foundation of any relationship. And, if your partner is able to tell you the truth about that whole snoring thing, then just imagine what else he's able to tell you the truth about. The possibilities are endless! You should be thankful and grateful for having an honest partner. Suppose your McDreamy was never able to tell you that you snore. You'd wake up and there he'd be—just watching you sleep. He'd always seem to get up hours before you. You'd soon realize that your McDreamy isn't sleeping over as much as he used to. You'd wonder what was wrong. You'd jump to conclusions . . . He's abandoning you, he's met someone else, he's allergic to your feather pillows . . . You'd drive yourself crazy! But, all of this is avoided when your Mc-Dreamy tells the truth. Although honesty in a relationship can sometimes hurt, it's better for both of you in the end. Your partner gets his sleep. And you get the satisfaction of knowing you picked a trustworthy guy.

Telling the truth isn't such an easy thing to do. It wouldn't be so important if it was simple. Still, we should all strive to be honest people. *Especially* in relationships. *Especially* if you're pregnant. Oh, dears, please don't try to hide the truth about *that*! Let me tell you more about what happened when Cristina failed to mention her pregnancy to her then-boyfriend, Dr. Burke. Not a happy time. Not a happy time at all . . .

I guess Cristina became pregnant pretty early on in her relationship with Burke. I mean, it felt like she had just started her internship and—the next thing I knew—Cristina was fighting for her life as she suffered from an ectopic pregnancy. It had to have been extraordinarily difficult for Seattle Grace's most ambitious surgical intern to be pregnant. Cristina was going to be a surgeon. And, she wasn't going to let *anything* get in the way of her goal. Motherhood was *not* in her immediate future. Which is why Cristina opted to terminate her pregnancy.

Indeed, it must've been a challenging time for the young intern. And to make matters worse, she was going through it all alone. Sure, she designated Meredith as her *person*, but she failed to tell the baby's father. Maybe Cristina was confused. Or scared. Or simply didn't need another opinion about what to do. Cristina is *very* set in her ways, so she was probably convinced that her decision was the best thing to do.

Cristina failed to tell Burke the truth. Which, according to Cristina, isn't lying. Hey, Burke never asked, right? So, Cristina just didn't tell him. She never technically "lied." But, *we*—meaning *you and I*—know better, right? We heal with love. So, we know a little bit more about honesty than I guess Cristina does. Sure, Cristina may have likened failing to tell Burke about her pregnancy to a "half-truth," but *we* know that "half-truths" are whole lies.

Sure, a lie takes care of the present. But, what about the future? Inevitably, a lie will complicate the future. Burke, for example, found out about his girlfriend's pregnancy under the worst of circumstances. Before she could terminate the pregnancy, Cristina's left fallopian tube burst, causing her to collapse. It's called an extra-uterine pregnancy and it's pretty scary. The doctors did everything they could, but they just couldn't save the tube. Burke quickly learned about the entire situation. Luckily, Cristina made a full recovery. I can't say that Burke did the same . . .

Of course, that wasn't the last of Cristina and Burke's dishonesty with each other. If Cristina was able to lie about her pregnancy, what else was she capable of lying about? How about when Burke "keyed" her?

Yes, one morning, I heard that Cristina woke up and found something pretty peculiar in her coffee cup. It was a key. *Burke's* key. To his *apartment*. Like he was asking Cristina to move in with him. It was supposed to be a big step in their relationship. Well, Cristina eventually accepted the key but, at the same time, kept a big secret. She never moved out of her apartment! Burke, of course, assumed that she did. Oh, Cristina. Enough with the "half-truths" and whole lies! In my opinion, Burke deserved to know about the pregnancy and he deserved to know whether Cristina totally, officially moved in with him. You can't live in two different places, right? Cristina could have made a commitment to her relationship by moving into Burke's place, but she didn't . . . which sent a very clear signal—wouldn't you agree?

You see, once you start lying in a relationship, it's very easy to fall into a vicious cycle of dishonesty and deceit. Where does it end? When do you stop telling lies and start telling the truth? It becomes blurry. And confusing. Pretty soon, you start involving other people in your lies. Which is even worse! You're no longer just affecting yourself, your partner and your relationship, you're now affecting those around you, too. (Hand tremors, anyone?)

Once again, I want to remind you—the next time you think about lying—think about the *future*. Because it *will* be affected. *Negatively*. I mean, did Cristina and Burke truly think the hand tremor scenario wouldn't eventually see the light of day? I doubt it. But they were just so caught up in the moment, so scared of losing everything, that they did what they had to do. They lied.

Finally, as you know, Cristina decided to tell the truth—before things had the chance to go really bad. And, Burke, naturally, felt betrayed. So what did Mr. Shaky Hands do? Well, he gave Cristina the silent treatment—which isn't a very healthy way to handle situations, mind you. Cristina happily participated. Neither of them talked for what seemed like years! Let me tell you, silent treatments don't solve anything. Sure, you're not talking so at least you're not lying. But you're not telling the truth either, which is exactly what you need to be doing!

I hate to say this, but, Cristina and Burke's relationship seemed doomed from the beginning. To me, at least. All of those lies, they're not good for anybody. And, well, look what happened when they started actually telling the truth—when Burke realized he wasn't in love with Cristina. When he realized he shouldn't be trying to change Cristina and mold her into something she just wasn't. Look what happened then—in that church, on the day of their wedding. Okay, I'll tell you what didn't happen: They didn't say "I do," that's for sure. I'll just leave it at that. For now.

My point is—a relationship, by definition, is based on trust. You should *always* tell the truth. Even though, sometimes, the truth hurts—it will *always* protect your future. I'll leave you with one final story about the importance of honesty. It involves Meredith, her boyfriend's ex-wife, and a whole lot of morphine. I suppose sometimes you've just got to be high off of morphine in order to be honest!

It was last year when Meredith came into work one morning—sick as a dog I tell ya! No, she didn't look so good. And, when she actually threw up at a nurse's station, everybody knew something was up. It was a pretty dramatic morning, to say the least. One of our patients practically blew his face off when he lit a cigarette in his hospital room. Yes, he really did. In case you don't know—cigarettes and hospitals with oxygen supplies just don't mix. Anyhoo—at the same time, just down the hallway, Mark showed up for his first day of work at Seattle Grace. That would be Derek's ex-best friend Mark and Addison's ex-lover Mark. And then, of course, there was little ol' Meredith, tossing her cookies right there in plain view of everyone. Like I said: *dramatic!*

Word spread pretty quickly that Meredith was pregnant. Oh, those gossip hounds—they'll get you every time. I overheard Addison call it an "adulterous love child." Well, fast forward an hour or so when *everyone* was relieved that Meredith was not, in fact, pregnant. She just suffered from appendicitis. No big deal!

Now, if you've ever been in the same boat as Meredith, you'd know that an appendicitis hurts like the dickens! You need morphine. Lots and lots of morphine. Which is exactly what Meredith got. Well, she actually got a whole lot more than she bargained for . . . Because, pretty soon, Meredith was spilling her guts to *Addison*, of all people . . .

That's correct. According to a nurse who overheard the entire conversation, Meredith—high as a kite—was having a personal, in-depth conversation with none other than Addison Shepherd . . . the woman who once took Mer's McDreamy, McDog and McLife. Conversations like *that* do not happen so often around here. The funny thing was, Meredith was speaking to her ex-boyfriend's ex-wife with such honesty and kindness . . .

Meredith was hurt when Derek picked Addison. And, at that point, Meredith was confused as to whether Derek was "the one." The young intern was actually asking the world-renowned, leggy and fabulous neonatal surgeon for some honest *advice*. So maybe it was just the morphine talking. Still, Meredith was able to get at least one great thing out of that honest conversation: *closure*.

It was hard for Meredith to tell Addison the truth. But after she said it, she felt better. Thereafter, the women's mutual respect for one another grew stronger. They were actually able to share some laughs and become somewhat "friendly." It was a beautiful thing. That simple, honest conversation *healed* both of those women. Why? Because they finally looked at one another and told the truth.

Sure, in the present moment, the truth can oftentimes sting. But—more importantly—in the future, you'll discover that the truth will almost always heal. So, from this day on, I want you to make a promise to me—Dr. Sydney Heron—that you will *always* tell the truth. Even if you have to get high off of morphine to do so! Okay, not really. Well . . . *maybe* as a last resort!

Now, while we're on the subject of truth in relationships, let's look a little deeper, shall we? Let's turn our attention to one of the worst, most harmful and deceitful kinds of dishonesty . . . Cheating, adultery, infidelity, unfaithfulness—call it what you will. Remember what I said about healing with love? It will help you through *any* situation, even this one . . .

CHAPTER NINE

Cheating Is for Losers. And You Are a Winner. Even if Your Man Did Cheat on You with a Supermodel.

"Respect yourself and others will respect you."

—CONFUCIUS

LUCKY FOR ME, I've never been cheated on. At least, I don't think I've been cheated on. I would know, though. When it comes to women's intuition—I've got *a lot* of it. Anyhoo, one thing I know *for sure*, however, is that I have never, ever cheated on a boyfriend. It's just not my cup of tea. That's not to say there haven't been any temptations. We're *all* going to face those. I've just been successful at ignoring them . . .

Back when I was with Derek, for example, I faced quite the temptation: McSteamy. Oh yes, I could tell by the way he was looking at me—McSteamy was *interested*. He wanted *all of this*. But, you know, I was seeing Derek. I was in a committed relationship. So, I couldn't pay McSteamy any attention. I blocked him, his chiseled jaw and his bulging biceps out of my mind. I didn't think about any of that. Out of respect for my boyfriend, Derek, of course. And, besides, did we really need another love triangle around this place? I mean, just pencil Derek/Sydney/Mark next to Callie/George/Izzie and Meredith/Derek/Addison and

Ellis/Richard/Adele and Ava/Alex/Lexie . . . No thank you! Like I said, *I'm* a faithful kind of gal.

If you're reading this right now and are guilty of infidelity, please know that I'm not judging you. That just means you have a lot of healing with love to do, and I'm here to support you on your journey. You're George. Or Addison. Or Richard. You've struggled with cheating. You've wrestled with your conscience. And you've probably already paid the price. Even though I haven't experienced your struggle firsthand, I can still help you heal your adulterous battle wounds with *love*.

For those of you reading this right now who fall on the *other* side of the fence . . . You're Callie. Or Derek. Or Adele. You've been cheated on. You've been deceived. You've been hurt. To all of *you*, I say, come along with Syd and heal with love!

And, to the rest of you . . . Those who have been fortunate enough to have never dealt with this thing called "cheating," maybe you have a best friend who needs a shoulder to cry on. A best friend who has been hurt by someone they love. Or, a best friend who has hurt someone they love and now feels really, really guilty. Go ahead, help him heal with love! Just don't get drunk with him and end up sleeping with him in the process . . . That'd make you Izzie. And, you don't want to be Izzie in that particular situation . . .

Alright, let me start by saying this: No one is a "cheater." Yes, you may have "cheated," but you can't let that define you. Every single one of us is flawed. Remember that bit? We all make mistakes. And, when we do, what are we supposed to do? Come on . . . You know this . . . This was several chapters back . . . That's right! We hug it out! Of course, some people go on "hug it out overload" and take that principle to a whole new level . . . They end up sleeping with their best friend. I don't recommend this.

I heard a pesky little rumor around here concerning George's restraint when he decided to hug it out with Izzie not too long ago. You see, George had been having some problems with his marriage for quite some time. All was not well. As a matter of fact, I think George and Callie's marriage began to struggle the day they showed up at SGH wearing wedding rings! They had eloped and gotten married at the Church of Elvis in Vegas while on a short vacation. Well, many people thought the whole thing was a bit odd . . . *especially* George's friends. They felt that George hadn't been with Callie for all that long, so . . . The whole marriage just seemed rather abrupt and sudden. But, George assured his friends that he was happy with Callie. After all, she understood him.

Still, I, for one, could tell that something wasn't right from day one. I was trying not to think negatively, so I gave them the benefit of the doubt. But, then I heard Callie call George's friends "weird and judgey." At that point, I guess George was totally distraught about not knowing Callie's middle name. Callie thought George was having a full-blown panic attack about it! Little did she know, however, that George had been exposed to a patient's toxic blood just minutes earlier, so, the panic attack was quite real! Anyhoo—Callie didn't like being out of her and George's Vegas bubble. Callie thought George's friends were getting to her husband. *Izzie*, in particular.

Yes, Izzie was perhaps the most judgmental about George's hasty nuptials. Let's see—she made fun of the size of Callie's wedding ring (even if it was unintentional), she questioned George's decision (openly, in front of Callie), and she snickered when Callie's middle name was finally revealed ("Iphegenia," which *I* think is beautiful). George finally put Izzie's concerns to rest when he confessed that he was, in fact, in love with Callie. Sure, Izzie was relieved, but only for a short period of time. She was still worried that George had made a huge mistake when he took those vows with Callie.

I suppose Izzie had a right to be concerned for her best friend. After all, it had been one heck of a year for George. Right before George decided to take the plunge and marry Callie Iphegenia Torres, his father passed. The young intern was completely thrown. He was hysterical, distressed. I got the feeling that Izzie always felt that George married Callie as a way of dealing with his father's death. Which, of course, cannot be good for a marriage, because, well—what happens when George has to finally "wake up" and discover the magnitude of what it really meant to be "married?"

For a period of time, it really was Callie vs. Izzie. And, of course, George was caught in the middle. His wife vs. his best friend. He was going to have to make a choice. Callie resented Izzie and vice versa. Their feud came to a head when George accidentally told Izzie a very vital, very secret piece of information about Callie: She was an heiress. That's right—loaded. A true rich girl.

Callie was mortified when she discovered that George had told Izzie her secret. It was a betrayal. For Callie, it felt as if George had made his choice—and he picked Izzie. It wasn't a great feeling . . . Your husband telling another woman *your* secrets. In Callie's mind, she was *sure* that Izzie was attracted to George. Callie thought that Izzie was trying to steal George away from her. She didn't know what to do.

And, then, it happened . . . The sex between Izzie and George. From what I gathered, the George/Izzie sex came about as abruptly as the George/Callie wedding. They were drinking. They were laughing. George was confiding in his best friend about his marriage. He told Izzie all about his marital strife. He was, in fact, trying to heal with love. However, being a newbie at that sort of thing, George healed with *too much* love. And then he hugged it out. Oh, boy, did he hug it out!

No one heard about George and Izzie's affair for a while. They were able to keep it a secret. But, as we all know, secrets have a way of coming out. And that one came out with a bang!

All I know is that I was standing in line in the cafeteria, waiting for my burrito, when my friend Janet started telling me about "Seattle Grace's First Ever Smackdown." Supposedly, the entire hospital had been buzzing about it all morning. Callie vs. Izzie. In the flesh! Some people were taking bets, but I don't gamble, so I refrained. (Between you and I, though, my money would've been on Callie for sure.)

Well, the match was to take place at noon, right there in the cafeteria. Sure enough, the clock struck 12 and Callie waltzed in. I saw Izzie getting ready—stretching, warming up, taking her earrings out—what was this, *Street Fighter*? Anyhoo—Callie sauntered over to Izzie, stared her down, and left . . . Somebody said Callie forfeited, but I don't think the woman was there to fight. Ready to talk? Maybe. Ready to rumble? No way.

Soon after, Callie and George ended their tumultuous marriage and divorced. As for George and Izzie, they actually attempted to make it work. That one drunken night meant more than just sex to them. They believed they had deeper feelings for one another. I heard that they refused to have sex again until George's divorce was finalized. And, after George was officially single, he and Izzie tried to have a *real* relationship. It had its own problems, however . . . Problems that will be analyzed in a later chapter . . .

As for Callie, she was ultimately able to forgive George. She was able to let go. Not immediately, but eventually. If you're ever in Callie's position, you're going to want revenge. You're a woman scorned. It's just a natural instinct. But, like the proverb states, "Before you begin on the journey of revenge, dig two graves." Revenge, you see, is a waste of time. Don't bother expending all of that energy on something so futile. Revenge is negative. And, if you heal with love, you don't mess with the negative. Instead, focus on something positive: yourself. Decide to let go. Forgive and forget. You'll see: Forgiveness really is the best kind of revenge.

Like I said earlier, we all make mistakes. So, if you're ever in George's or even Izzie's position, you can't afford to torture yourself over a decision you regret. George's marriage may have very well been over long before he slept with Izzie. He and Callie were never supposed to get married. It still doesn't make what George did right. But, now, George is able to learn from his mistakes . . .

People change and they don't always tell one another. George was a different person after his father's death. And he was a different person the night he decided to sleep with Izzie. The same goes for Callie—it didn't seem like she was ever truly happy in her marriage. She was a different person the night of her wedding than she was the day she told George that Izzie was attracted to him.

Here's the thing: Maybe you don't always get what you pay for, but you always—no matter what—pay for what you get. It's called karma. And, boy, it can be a real bitch (pardon my French)! When Addison slept with Mark, moved to Seattle, won Derek back, and stole Meredith's McDog and McLife—what did she get in return? Poison oak where nobody wants to get poison oak. As for Izzie and George? They got bad sex. So, whether it's poison oak on your va-jay-jay, bad sex, or even putrid goo all over your pretty blue scrubs—you're *going* to get what's coming to you. It's just another way we learn from our mistakes.

For those who cheat and for those who are cheated on, it

comes down to one thing for both: self-respect. In other words: self-love. Don't forget to love yourself if your man (or woman) ever cheats on you. Nobody can make you feel inferior without your permission. Forget about punishment and revenge . . . You've got to let go. Don't waste another ounce of energy on the someone who's cheating on you or the someone who that someone is cheating on you with. Make sense? Good! Whether the "other woman" is a former supermodel or not—just remember— she's going to get what's coming to her. And *you* don't need to be a part of it.

The same goes for those who cheat. Remember: Self-respect is self-love! So, respect and love yourself enough to accept the fact that you made a mistake. You're human. You're allowed to make some errors in your judgments. But *learn* something from those errors and don't do it again. So your co-worker is calling you a home wrecker. So your neighbors are calling you names my publisher won't allow me to type. It's not what they call you—it's what you answer to . . . Don't harp on the situation. Respect and love yourself enough and, sooner or later, others will begin to respect and love you, too. And, once *that* happens—I can guarantee you—you'll be healed.

HERONISM

I know what *you* need: A self-esteem upgrade! A morale boost! That's right—there's no better weapon to use against the nasty little force of temptation than a good ol' promotion in the confidence department!

Confidence, you see, improves your level of self-respect. And, as you know, self-respect allows you to look temptation right in the eye and say, "No, thank you!" It will help you make better, more rational choices (such as, the decision to not cheat on your wife). Here's a quick little exercise to build a stronger, healthier, more confident *you*:

Okay, pick a hero, any hero. Who, in your mind, is just the bee's knees? Who do you look up to? Who would you like to emulate? It can be someone you know—a co-worker, a boss, a friend, a parent . . . Or, it can be someone you don't know— the president, the humanitarian celebrity that just returned from Africa, the neighbor who brought you a fruitcake when you moved in . . . Hey, it can even be someone who's not real—a comic book hero, a literary figure, a movie character . . . Just pick somebody!

Once you've chosen your hero, write down *all* of the quali- ties you admire in that individual. Take your time. Now, in the comfort of your own home (without anyone looking), pretend you're that hero. Walk like him. Pour yourself a glass of water and drink like him. Think of a commonly used phrase he'd say and start to talk like him. *Become* him. Do this for about thirty minutes.

Next, take a seat and visualize yourself (as your hero) in any particular predicament you've previously faced. How would *your hero* have acted differently in the *same situation*? Would *he* have slept with your best friend after getting drunk? Would *he* have gone to Vegas and gotten married after your father died? Ask yourself those questions honestly. Then, end this exercise by repeating your hero's commonly used phrase.

Now, how do you feel? More confident? More like *your hero*? Good! That's the point! If you do this exercise often enough, the next time you're in a sticky situation, you'll auto- matically begin to "act" like your hero. It's true! You'll have tons of self-respect. You'll have an extraordinary level of self- esteem. You really won't be able to give in to *any* temptation!

Take it from me—I consistently visualize myself as Richard Webber (my own personal hero). And, when I'm facing a temptation or involved in some kind of mess, I often find myself acting *just like him*. I'll roam the halls with my head held high! I'll have all the confidence in the world! I'll yell, "That's why I'm the Chief! That's why I'm the Chief!" Oh, boy, I'm telling you—this exercise *really* works! Try it and see!

CHAPTER TEN

You're Not My Girlfriend, Okay?

*"Human beings, like plants, grow in the soil
of acceptance, not in the atmosphere of rejection."*

—JOHN POWELL,
English jurist

I HAVE A CONFESSION to make . . . This may come as a surprise to you—and to any of my peers who are reading this—but, here goes . . . When I first applied to medical school, I was *rejected*. I know—can you believe it?! Those ghouls had the nerve to say "no" to *me*? What—was my essay too generalized? Did I say something unintelligent or flippant during my interview? Was there a glitch in the system?

Upon receiving that rejection letter, I searched for answers. And, when I couldn't find any, I became depressed. My dream was crushed. I was never going to become a surgeon, I thought. I remember lying in bed for a full three days until it finally dawned on me . . .

I needed to make my haters my motivators.

And so, I did just that.

I started interning at a local hospital. I became involved with a medical nonprofit organization. I traveled to South America, Europe and Africa, where—in Zimbabwe—I saw a boy who had been in a month-long coma finally wake up. In short, that entire

year changed my life. I remained determined to become a surgeon. One admissions board was *not* going to deter the future
Dr. Sydney Heron.

So, exactly one year after reading that silly letter of rejection,
I applied to a *better* medical school and . . . Drum roll please . . .
I was accepted!

Oh, the satisfaction I felt at that moment in time was immea-
surable. Just for kicks, I wrote a long letter to the admissions
board that once rejected me. I outlined all of my achievements
and thanked them. Yes, I did! Without their rejection, you see, I
would've never been able to experience such an amazing year. I
would've never been able to meet such amazing people all over
the world. I would've never been able to become the doctor I am
today.

Rejection is never an easy pill to swallow . . . *especially* when it
comes to relationships. Nope, it's not really any fun at all. Everyone goes through it, though. And, we all have to remember that
rejection *is* actually good for something: strengthening our resolve. That, of course, is how we become successful in both life
and love. Reminding yourself about this simple idea will help
you heal after any kind of rejection.

Which brings us to another pop quiz! Pencils ready!

Which of the following sounds like the *best* cure for the rejection blues?

A. Wallowing in bed while eating strawberry ice cream and
   wishing you could be treated like a freakin' lady.
B. Tequila, of course. Lots and lots of tequila.
C. Sleeping with a skanky syph nurse to get even.
D. Sleeping with *several* skanky syph nurses to get even.
E. Road trip to sunnier climes—where you can get away from

all the drama and visit your med-school friend who happens to be a fertility specialist at a medical co-op.

This one is tricky, right?

Well, "E" is the correct answer. Let's look at the incorrect choices first . . .

Okay, you don't want to wallow. If you're wallowing, then you're not strengthening your resolve. And that's exactly what you need to be doing. As for tequila—well, we know where that stuff gets you (re-read the very first chapter, silly). And, whether it's one skanky syph nurse or five of them, you're not going to get even with *anybody*. You're only going to miss opportunities and chances with the former lingerie model who commanded you to "take off your freakin' pants" in the middle of a Code Black or the pregnant, amnesiac Jane Doe you rescued from a ferry crash or a friend's younger sister who you seem to have *a lot* in common with. But more on all of that in a minute . . .

Oh, I hoped you picked "E." Because, that's the only real solution of the bunch when the man you just slept with makes you realize that there's *gotta* be something better for you out there when he tells you, "You're not my girlfriend, okay?"

So, you may have guessed—this last scenario *really* happened at Seattle Grace. And, that line was *really* uttered on one cold night just a little while ago. It was Alex who said it. The Bad Boy! After Alex muttered those words—to Addison—well, *she* was never really the same.

Once upon a time, Alex was Addison's very gynie-reluctant intern. Oh, he hated being on Addie's service. He "didn't do vaginas. Not as a doctor, anyway." His words, not mine. Well, what started as a mutual dislike for one another quickly turned into attraction. I've heard several stories from nurses who supposedly saw Addison and Alex "almost kiss." Some have al-

legedly witnessed a few rather awkward, nervous glances between the two as well. Well, take it from me, when the nurses
start talking at SGH, then it's usually true. They're like our very
own tabloid journalists.

Anyhoo, Addison and Alex's relationship seemed to be on
simmer for quite a while. It was teacher and pupil. A world-
renowned surgeon and a first year—extremely cocky—intern. I
don't think anything "major" happened between them . . . at
first . . . But, when Alex started showing his unusual side of ten-
derness and compassion for a Jane Doe, Addison couldn't help
but take notice . . .

Days earlier, a horrible ferry crash had occurred. Oh, it was
awful. Bodies were piling up in the ER. It was a real tragedy, let
me tell you. We were actually completing our emergency training that day, so it was a true surprise when an *actual* emergency
took place. Many of us were caught off guard. Teams were sent
to the accident scene. There, Alex apparently found a pregnant
woman trapped underneath debris on the ferry dock. He hero-
ically rescued her and brought her into the hospital. It was determined that the woman suffered massive injuries and couldn't
remember anything, so she became a Jane Doe.

It was completely touching to see the close attention that
Alex paid to his patient. He was constantly checking on her.
Whenever Alex did so, Jane Doe was visibly relieved. Alex was
the only person that Jane seemed to respond to. He would talk to
her, console her and explain to her what was really going on.
Alex actually helped give Jane a face and a real name. When
Mark needed to reconstruct Jane's face, it was Alex who kept
Jane calm and got her to pick the face she wanted. *Ava.* According to Alex, *Ava* was her real name. When I heard about that, I
was truly impressed with Alex. He certainly seemed to have
come a long way from his frat-boy days.

I wasn't the only one who was impressed . . . Like I said, Addison took notice, too. And, when Ava went into labor, that's when the fireworks *really* started . . . Oh, yes, that was the day I was tending to leaking spinal fluid guy. Still, I heard what happened from the nurses . . .

Addison and Alex needed to perform an emergency C-section on Ava. It was a scary procedure. Ava must've been terrified for both herself and her baby. Still, Alex kept her calm. Kept her breathing. He was Ava's rock. Thanks to Alex's care and warmth, the surgery was a success. Ava gave birth to a beautiful baby girl!

After the operation, Addison cornered Alex and demanded to know if Alex had become too personally involved. She had never seen Alex so attentive, so caring, so loving. Alex denied it, but Addison didn't; she pushed her intern into the closest on-call room and, well, by now you know what happens in our on-call rooms!

Fast forward to the end of the day when Addison found Alex sitting in the lobby, studying for his intern test. That's when Addison invited Alex back to her hotel room. To study and . . . Well, that's when Alex supposedly said his line: "You're not my girlfriend, okay?"

Alex, you see, had studying to do. That's why he was there, at SGH, to become a surgeon. Addison—I'm sure—was shocked. Had she ever been rejected before? Like *that*? Of course, Addison began to wonder why she herself was there at SGH. She had already lost what felt like the love of her life. Her prospects of being named Seattle Grace's next Chief of Surgery looked dim. Her intern had just *rejected* her. And—perhaps most importantly— Addison felt about as bad as a manwhore . . . Let me explain . . .

The sixty-day sex bet. You see, Addison had told Mark (SGH's resident manwhore) that if he could go sixty days— about two full months—without sex, then Addison would make a real go at their relationship. Addison knew that Mark wasn't going to last for that long, even though—deep in her heart—she probably would've liked it if Mark was able to hold out. Alas, it just wasn't a goal that a manwhore was capable of reaching. Mark confessed to Addison that he lost the bet, and so it was confirmed. But what did that say for Addison? She had promised Mark if he wasn't allowed to have sex, then neither was she. Yet, Addison's secret on-call rendezvous with Alex happened that afternoon. So, in the end, Addison wasn't able to hold out, either. She lost the sixty-day sex bet as well. Yes, it seemed that Addison was no better than a manwhore.

Addison, perhaps for the first time in her life, had been rejected so severely—by Derek, by Alex, by Mark and—at that point—by *herself,* that she needed to get away. Oh, she desperately needed to get away. So, the very next day, everyone was surprised to find out that Addison was *gone.* Road trip! Down to Los Angeles, where Addison's best friend worked at a medical co-op. It was a short visit, but it was so good for Addison to just get away from all of the drama. She was strengthening her resolve, discovering what else was out there. Apparently, there was an empty office and a whole new life for her down in L.A.

Addison returned to SGH rejuvenated. She had a new outlook on life. Things seemed to be clear now . . . Derek is in love with Meredith. Alex wants Ava. And, for Mark, well . . . Once a manwhore, always a manwhore. Then, as Addison probably predicted, Richard rejected her for the Chief of Surgery job. That decision made up her mind . . . Addison needed to leave SGH once and for all . . .

So, she left. And, we'll miss her. But, in part, do you realize what Addison owes her new life to? That's right: *rejection.* It sounds silly, I know, but, if Addison hadn't gone through all of that rejection, then she never would've seen what Los Angeles had to offer. We can learn something from Addie. I know I did! And, that is, there comes a time in all of our lives when we have to stop regretting the past and stop fearing the future. At some point, we just have to take the plunge and see what happens. Forget the past. Forget our fears. Forget our plans. *Embrace*—don't worry about—the future. Whatever happens will happen.

Now, by no means am I telling you that the next time somebody rejects you, skip town and move far, far away. You'll have to decide that for yourself. The important thing to remember is that you cannot let rejection beat you upside your head with a crazy stick. You've got to persevere. There's no other way to be successful.

Look, all of us are going to deal with rejection differently. Some travel to Zimbabwe to visit sick children and write about them in extraordinary medical school application essays. Others pack up their bags, move to the land of sunshine and start anew. Whatever works, I say, as long as you are not hurting others because of your own constant fear of rejection. Oh, where'd that come from, you ask? Well, you know about Alex, don't you?

My young healers, Alex is the kind of person to look out for. And, if you ever find yourself in a relationship with this bad boy, you're going to want to pay special attention to this next part.

Alexes are very hard to understand and figure out. They are very complex, emotionally stunted human beings. They're impossible to dissect, so there's really no use trying. I'll just say this: Alexes are so used to the idea of rejection that they'll spend their lives rejecting people, things and themselves because they're so comfortable with it. I mean, it makes sense, right? We all like to do what's comfortable. So, if rejection is what we're used to, rejection is what we're going to do. It's a vicious, never-ending cycle. The good news, however, is that it's something love can heal!

I'm talking about loving yourself. If you love yourself, *Alex*, then you're not going to want to miss out on those opportunities that are going to change your life. If you know an Alex, *tell him that*. There's nothing worse than losing a chance to get better. The Alex I know, for example, rushed his little tush back to the hospital the day Ava was leaving for good. Hours earlier, Ava was supposedly asking Alex for a reason to stay. She was in love with him. But Alex, being an Alex, did what was comfortable and rejected her. It's a habit for those Alexes, let me tell you. Anyway, after having a conversation with Addison—a woman who knows a thing or two about missed opportunities—Alex hurried back to Ava's hospital room to see her one last time but it was too late . . . Ava was gone. And Alex missed his chance . . .

Of course, Ava wasn't gone for good. Yes, Ava's made a few surprise appearances back at SGH in recent weeks. From what I gather, Alex and Ava are still secretly sleeping together—even though Ava is married (please, Ava, read Chapter Nine) and Alex has started sleeping with Lexie, Meredith's half-sister. And, guess what? Even though Alex and Lexie seem like kindred spirits—they both have their issues, they both have alcoholic dads, etc., etc.—Alex is *still* doing his share of rejecting. You see, Alex is either rejecting a woman or rejecting his feelings for a woman. I suppose only time will tell whether Lexie will continue to put up with her bad boy's crap!

Boy, those Alexes . . . Like I said—they're tough nuts to crack! Just remember: They need to first love themselves before they're capable of loving anyone else. Sounds a bit trite, but it's the truth!

The French writer and physician Louis-Ferdinand Céline once said, "I think all great innovations are built on rejections." I do too, Louis. You see, if you're unable to gain acceptance—in either life or love—then, by all means, do whatever it takes to jump back on the horse. Think of rejection as just another opportunity to love yourself. You'll soon discover that you're stronger, more powerful and more determined than ever to get what you want. That's the thing—being stronger, more powerful and more determined makes it *that* much harder for rejection to occur. It's how you grow. At that point, you're ready, able and capable to conquer the world! You and only you hold the key to your success and happiness. That's what I realized. That's what Addison realized. And that's what *you* can realize, whether you're an Alex or not . . .

CHAPTER ELEVEN

Law of Attraction—
The ManWhore

"There is a charm about the forbidden
that makes it unspeakably desirable."

—MARK TWAIN

I'M PRETTY SURE you know the type. Come on, ladies. The face, the hair, the voice, the body . . . The way he looks at you when you ask for a consult. The way his eyes pierce your soul and bring your blood to a rolling boil. The way his fingers linger on yours when you hand him a patient chart. They're not soft—they're manly, masculine, well-worn . . . Oh yeah, he's lived. He's seen a lot in his day. All of that experience—He knows what to do . . . He knows how to please . . .

Alright, before I get carried away, I'm talking about the man-whore. You know, the kind of guy who sleeps with his best friend's wife, answers transcontinental booty calls *with a run*, lists "one night stands" as his all-time favorite hobby, makes sixty-day sex bets, asks if you want his "pickle" and angers the nurses after using the same "techniques" over and over and over . . . Sound familiar? Thought so. You know a manwhore, too.

They're nasty little creatures, aren't they? Somehow, man-whores *always* seem to get under your skin (or into your pants) and end up getting exactly what they want. How do they do it?

Well, that's the million dollar question. Nobody knows for sure . . . All I know is that they like to saunter out of steamy showers and make tiny bath towels look oh-so-good. But that's just part of their charm . . . part of their evil ways and their master plan.

The truth is—the manwhore has been around for quite some time. Ever since the beginning of man, actually, the manwhore has been hard at work. Womanizers, playboys, players, Casanovas, Don Juans—call them what you will—their lineage goes way, way back. Needless to say, they've spent *a lot* of time studying the subject of temptation and, therefore, have been able to master the art of seduction. Sadly, there has never been a shortage of manwhores, nor has there ever been a lack of the women who—try as they might—simply cannot resist them. It seems like the manwhore is an old problem.

Now, I've mentioned SGH's resident manwhore, Mark, many times already. Well, I'm devoting an entire chapter to him. I figured a man like Mark has *mucho* healing with love to do. I mean, all of those late nights and one night stands, none of those things can *really* be satisfying for manwhores, can they? No way, Jose. Believe it or not, they actually have feelings. So it is my belief that even manwhores deserve something better than booty calls and furtive meet-me-in-the-on-call-room-in-five-minutes glances. Manwhores are people, too!

So, if you are, in fact, a manwhore, well . . . congratulations! At least you just admitted it to yourself. And, that's the first step on the road to manwhore recovery. You want *more* for yourself, right? It's okay, my dear manwhore, you can admit it. Maybe you want to press "ignore" the next time your phone lights up and it's "hot blonde peds nurse." Good for you! (Baby steps, baby steps.) Or, perhaps you want a steady girlfriend? A wife? Children, one day? Maybe you want to be named Chief but, in your heart, you know that won't happen because nobody takes you seriously. So you want respect?

Well, manwhore, if you want respect, you're going to have to give respect. You're going to have to respect *yourself* enough to say no to your next booty call. And you're going to have to respect others if you want them to respect you. It's just that simple.

I know, it seems like a lot to ask for, manwhore. Yes, it will be a change for you. But, change is good. Remember, you want something *more*. And, if you keep doing things like you've always done, then all you're going to get is what you've already got. So, I suggest you find a new hobby. Something other than *women*. Once you start respecting yourself and others, then your new pastime will come pretty easy to you. Just wait . . .

You, manwhore, are a special person. And, special people have *two*—count 'em *two*—new life mantras. You remember number one, right? "When in doubt, just hug it out." Well, in addition to looking into a mirror and saying *that* every morning, I want you, manwhore, to also say: "I am a man of substance." As a matter of fact, say it with me *right now*. "I am a man of substance." Again! "I am a man of substance." Very good! Listen, if you continue to say that phrase every morning and really believe in yourself, then you will, in fact, become a "man of substance." As a matter of fact, SGH's very own resident manwhore has been putting his new mantra to the test very recently . . .

It all began when Mark (like you, manwhore) decided he wanted something *more*. And, in this particular case, it was Seattle Grace's new cardiothoracic surgeon, Dr. Erica Hahn, that Mark wanted. You see, Mark was thoroughly impressed with Erica's surgical skills and technique ever since she started here. I overheard him one day commenting on Erica's "beautiful" hands. The finesse, the sophistication, the craftsmanship—he was going on and on, let me tell you!

Erica is an extremely talented surgeon. She's also an extremely interesting choice for Mark. Why? Because Erica was not interested in Mark *at all*. In fact, she seemed to be immune to his manwhorish ways. Erica, bless her heart, even told Mark that she was not interested. Yes, Mark seemed to have met his match.

Erica, you see, was a *woman* of substance. She had the ability to recognize Mark's game from the beginning and refused to take part. At first, Erica's reluctance toward anything having to do with Mark amused the manwhore. They would squabble. They would banter. They would diss one another. For Mark, it was all a source of entertainment. But, when Mark realized Erica was serious—she *really* didn't want anything to do with him—Mark decided that he himself would become a man of substance in his own right.

Mark, of course, is still working on it. You too, manwhore, will see that becoming "a man of substance" doesn't just happen overnight. You'll struggle. You'll think the world is against you and you're just "misunderstood." But, sooner or later, you'll forget your past ways and embrace your new future . . . You'll graduate from manwhore status and become a full-fledged, bona fide man of substance. And, when you do it, don't thank little ol' me. Thank *yourself!*

Now let's turn our attention to the other half of you reading this chapter: the women affected by manwhores day in and day out.

Like I said earlier, the manwhore is an old problem. And, like all old problems, it requires a *new* solution. Well, lucky for you, I've figured it out. Here goes . . . After witnessing Mark sleep his way through half of this hospital and noticing Erica's handling of the species, I'd like to introduce the following answer: *boundaries*. Yes, the new solution to the old problem of the manwhore lurking in the shadows is . . . *setting boundaries*.

"No, Mark, I *do not* want your pickle."

"No, Mark, I *will not* accompany you to the on-call room."

Or, my personal favorite: "You *cannot* buy me a drink, Mark. You disgust me. You repulse me. You disappoint me. I'm giving you the cold shoulder. My shoulder is actually frigid. Feel it. No, don't. So, goodbye, Mark. Stop talking to me. And just stop talking to me." <Storm off.>

See? It's all about *boundaries*. Erica seems to be the boundary master. She was able to *convincingly* tell Mark that she was absolutely *not* interested. The next time a manwhore approaches you and asks if you want to go back to his place, take a cue from Erica . . . Just say no!

Sadly, people are more comfortable with old problems than new solutions. So it's going to be hard, ladies. But, I want you to *try* to resist the temptation. Think of every second of resistance like a small victory. You want to win, right? Well, tell yourself that you can abstain and—guess what—you *will* abstain. The power of positive thinking really works! So his muscles look awfully protective and his musk is making your toes curl—who cares?! You're not paying attention to any of that because you, my dear, are setting boundaries and saying no! Yes, it will take strength. Yes, it will take courage. Yes, Mark may feel and smell really good, but it's just not right. You're better than that. And you deserve better than that.

Okay, let's say you're not strong or courageous enough to resist the manwhore's temptation. You're not going to feel very good about yourself in the morning, are you? Do you think those nurses felt good about themselves the morning after? Of course not! They had to form a union—NUAMS (Nurses United Against Mark Sloan)—to get over their manwhore crushes! Do you think Addison felt okay after continuing to sleep with Mark when he joined the staff of SGH? No, silly! It ultimately played a part in her decision to move out of Seattle and down to Los Angeles. And, do you think Callie felt alright after bedding Mark practically immediately after she broke up with George (the very *first* time, way before they got married)? *I don't think so.*

None of those women solved any problems by having sex with Mark, our friendly neighborhood manwhore. If anything, the deed just complicated matters. They were left feeling incredibly guilty (about Derek, about George, about being just another nurse who fell victim to McSteamy's commonly used techniques). Those women were left with a decreased level of self-respect and the not-so-shiny-and-happy feeling that they were just another notch on Mark's bedpost.

And, believe me, those notches? There are *many* of them. Hundreds! Thousands? Maybe. Who knows for sure? I don't!

So perhaps you decide to sleep with a manwhore as a last resort. Maybe you think one night of passion with the man of your dreams will fill some void in your life or solve some problem. You say to yourself, "Lots of ladies have been there. The manwhore is obviously a popular choice. Sleeping with him can't be *that* bad, can it? Maybe it will actually be good for me, then." Right? Wrong!

You're not on the right road just because it's a well-beaten path. And, believe me—bedding a manwhore is a well-beaten path. I mean, it's a pretty common occurrence, hence the whole manwhore label. Didn't your mother ever ask you, in that very berating tone she mastered, "If your friends told you to jump off a bridge, would you do it?" Well, the same logic goes for sleeping with a manwhore . . . Just because your friends are doing it doesn't mean you should. Don't jump on the bandwagon when everyone around you seems to be sleeping with a manwhore. Those guys, they're popular fellows indeed. But, just because something is popular doesn't mean it's good for you.

Alright, maybe I'm being too hard on the manwhores of the world. Sure, they've got their flaws, but who doesn't? After all, I've said it before and I'll say it again, we're all human. I'm sure every manwhore has at least one or two genuinely good things going for him. Hey, I bet some even go downtown on their weekends off to feed the poor. No? Not even one? Okay, perhaps there's a manwhore somewhere that actually forgoes a night at the bar to teach a child to read . . . What? No luck on that one either? Well, maybe there's a manwhore alive who's actually a good friend? I know one of those!

Mark has actually been a good friend to a couple of people around here. Mark and Meredith? They have a lot in common and they haven't even slept together, *ever* (go figure). Elsewhere, Mark and Derek have recently resurrected their friendship. Yes, it seems that Derek has finally truly forgiven Mark for sleeping with Addison. During the ferry crash disaster, Mark supported Derek when Meredith was unconscious. That was pretty big. Moreover, Mark and Derek have even been seen laughing and joking together. Oh, and more recently, Derek has given Mark some advice on Erica. Yes, it seems that Mark the manwhore has some true friends, indeed.

Remember that sixty-day sex bet I told you about in the last chapter? The one between Addison and Mark? Well, Mark told Addison that he lost the bet. He said that he wasn't able to hold out. Want to know a little-known secret around here? Mark was *lying*. He really didn't lose the bet and he actually *was* able to hold out. Yes, a nurse overheard Mark telling Derek the whole story. You see, Mark saw Addison and Alex walk out of an on-call room together, so he naturally assumed that the two had just had sex (which, as we all know now, is true). It was *Addison* who lost the bet, all by herself. But Mark actually went to Addison and told her that it was *him* who lost. He let her off the hook. It was Mark being compassionate, which was quite a new color for him. You know, that's a good sign for everybody . . . It means that manwhores really *can* change. And, they're not *all* bad.

Keep that in mind the next time you encounter a manwhore: He's not all bad. He just has some changing to do. However, do yourself a favor and hold off on sleeping with him until *after* he changes. Until then, set boundaries with the manwhore. Remember, just say no!

And, to all of you manwhores out there, bless your hearts. You're tired of everyone looking at you like a piece of meat. You're fed up with the nurses and their snarky little anti-you clubs. You're over women throwing themselves at your feet. Yes, all those on-call-room hookups and late night booty calls have gotten pretty stale. You're ready for a *real* challenge: you. That's right, you want to heal. You're trying to heal. You *need* to heal. It's just going to take time. And patience. Hey, good luck at becoming a man of substance! I have a feeling you're going to need it . . .

HERONISM

So, let me guess . . . There's a manwhore in your life and you're having a bit of trouble dealing with him. Am I right? Of course I am! Remember, the first thing you do with a manwhore is you set boundaries. An easy way to accomplish this is by writing the manwhore in your life a letter. That's right—a heartfelt, genuine Dear Manwhore that summarizes your feelings and, most importantly, outlines your boundaries.

Go ahead—in just a few paragraphs—tell your manwhore to keep his distance. Thank him for his interest and quickly dash his hopes of ever sleeping with you. Express your dissatisfaction with his trite pick-up lines, uncomfortable stares and troublesome advances. And, be sure to advise your man-whore that he will, no doubt, face severe consequences if he continues to drive you mad. Moreover, refrain from leaving your telephone number, home address or instant messenger name.

Write your letter today! Leave it in your manwhore's locker, at his doorstep or on the windshield of his car. I can practically guarantee that he'll be leaving you alone in no time!

Let's now turn our attention away from relationships with others and focus on one particular, very special, very important person . . . You! As I've said, love heals *all*. Why don't we take a deeper look at how the healing power of love can help you through any personal situation. Just remember, healing with love begins with *you* . . .

PART THREE

Healing Yourself
with Love

How to Heal After Cutting Your Boyfriend's LVAD Wire and Killing Him— All While Wearing Your Prom Dress

*"We must embrace pain and burn
it as fuel for our journey."*

—KENJI MIYAZAWA,
author

HEALING WITH LOVE—as you should know by now—
is a journey. And I'm not just talking about that hop,
skip and a jump down the block to your neighborhood conve-
nience store or that leisurely stroll across the street to your local
Emerald City Bar. No, siree. I'm talking about that arduous yet
truly fulfilling voyage that begins deep within your heart and
travels through every single organ, bone and vessel in your body.
Yeah, *that* one. The journey you begin dark, twisty and damaged—
and, magically, through the awesome power of love, end up
bright, shiny and *healed*.

Well, comrades, this journey never ends. And that's the honest to goodness truth! I, for example, have been traveling down
Heal with Love Drive for many, many years now. It's my own
personal Great Expedition. And, it's *quite* a scenic trip. I've jour-
neyed through desolate neighborhoods only to find villages of
wealth and abundance. Traveled beyond towns of depression

and reached cities of hope. Passed tiny, wretched landmarks before finally reaching grand, colorful monuments. By land, by sea, by air, I've gone from famine to feast, weak to strong, bleak and coarse to lush and refined! My journey has been exciting, rewarding and educational, but—most of all—it's been *my own*.

Here's the thing: No two journeys will ever be the same. Yours will be unique to you and only you. Your experiences—the paths you take, the roadblocks you overcome, the scenic outlooks you enjoy—will be different from anyone else's. Why, you ask? Because we all start from a different place. My starting point—that is, when I decided to embark on my own personal heal with love journey—isn't the same as yours. At least, I hope not.

Remember that tremendously dark period of my life I mentioned to you way back in Chapter One? You don't? Well, let's just say, several years ago, I was not a very happy camper. I suppose now's as good a time as any to go ahead and get this out of the way. Okay, here's the beginning of *my* journey. Grab some tissues . . .

I was a first-year intern. The lowest of the low on the Seattle Grace totem pole. I had worked my little tush off to get there and, finally, I had made it. Yes, Sydney Heron had arrived. I admit, I was a wee bit intimidated. My colleagues—they seemed so smart and talented. It felt like they had everything already figured out. I mean, standing on one side of me was Dr. Bailey (the *pre-Nazi* Dr. Bailey) and, on the other, there was Callie (the *pre-ortho-doc-who-could-break-your-bones-and-kick-your-ass* Callie). We were all just surgical interns, yet *they* seemed so much wiser and stronger. They seemed to be in another league—I certainly didn't see them as *my* competition, to tell you the truth. They were *that* much better than little ol' me. If eight of us were going to switch to an easier specialty, five were going to crack under the pressure and two were going to be asked to leave, I was certain that it would be *me* who'd accomplish all three. First, I would switch specialties, then I would crack under the pressure, and then I would be asked to leave. As you can see, this was *pre-heal-with-love* Sydney. I wasn't such a positive thinker back then, was I?

Needless to say, my first year started out pretty tough. And it only got tougher. I endured heinous ridicule after being nick-named "007" (i.e., "license to kill"), I served my sentence of what felt like a lifetime of scut, and I sheepishly allowed my peers to walk all over me. Somehow, I managed to put on a brave face every single day. (Later, I realized that I was simply repressing *a whole lot* of anger.) However, all of that was *nothing* compared to what happened about six months into my first year . . .

We were inundated with patients in the ER that day. Imagine the typical SGH train wreck or ferry crash or dead baby bike race and you'll get a sense of just how crazy things were in the pit. My resident told me to go help out, and so I went, rather re-luctantly. I was just so tired! I was working on just *two* hours of sleep and the only thing I had eaten that day was half of an ap-ple. I simply couldn't bring myself to eat the cafeteria's blue plate lunch special—autopsy, anyone?

Anyhoo, there I was in the pit, weary bones and all, finishing up a bit of my all-time favorite pastime: sutures. Okay, bring a book! I could do sutures (or, stitches, in case you're not up on your medical lingo) in my sleep. They're not very exciting, let me tell you! My fingers were beginning to ache, so I decided to tuck my trusty suture kit away and troll the ER for something a tad more interesting. Lucky for me, I found it about three curtains down . . .

I pulled back the curtain and found an awfully cute, brown-haired, nine-year-old boy sitting with his mother. The boy's big, brown, puppy dog eyes were teary, but, he was being a brave little soldier. His tummy hurt. He had a fever. And, he was nauseous. I examined him and determined that this little boy had a touch of the stomach flu. Nothing serious! Nothing a bunch of rest, fluids and time wouldn't fix. Surprisingly, I was a bit happy that the boy's case wasn't surgical. He was so darn cute. And, I wasn't mentally or physically prepared for the OR at that particular moment in time . . . So, I pulled the closest resident over to confirm my diagnosis. Then, I sent the little boy, his viral gastroenteritis and his mother on their way. After that, the resident (who I hadn't really worked with prior to that day) instructed me to get back to my—what else—sutures!

Two days later, the little boy returned. Only, this time, he looked a lot worse and seemed to be in a lot more pain. His mother was frantic. I told my regular resident I had discharged the boy two days earlier after diagnosing him with the flu . . . That's when my resident stopped what he was doing, just for a second, stared at me, and said dryly, "You made a mistake. This boy's appendix has ruptured."

The color drained out of my face. How could I have missed that? Sure, appys are pretty commonly misdiagnosed, but—how could I have been so *stupid*? So *negligent*? Obviously, I wasn't allowed to scrub in on the surgery, so I hid in a supply closet on the third floor. Oh, how I remember that feeling . . . The shaking, the nausea, the way my skin was literally crawling. My "007" nickname was completely warranted. I deserved nothing but scut for the rest of my career. How could my peers respect me? Moreover, how could I respect myself? I didn't need to switch specialties—I had already cracked under the pressure. It was only a matter of time before they asked me to leave.

Four hours later—it was Dr. Bailey who found me in that supply closet. I think I had fallen asleep. Immediately, I asked her about the little boy. The awfully cute, brown-haired, nine-year-old boy whose big, brown, puppy dog eyes—Bailey cut me off with a slow shake of her head.

"They did everything they could. There was a complication . . ." And, I didn't hear the rest . . . I stood up, passed Bailey and walked out of that hospital. My career, *my life*—I felt—*everything* was over. At that point, little did I realize, my journey was only beginning . . .

I had a breakdown. A little boy lost his life because of *me*. It didn't matter, to me, that a senior resident confirmed my initial misdiagnosis. It didn't matter that the boy died of surgical complications that no doctor could have ever predicted. None of that provided any sort of comfort. This was *my* fault.

I stopped speaking to everyone I knew. I refused to come out of my home. I couldn't stop crying. I was in hell. Now, I can tell you, that if you're ever in that position, if you ever feel that kind of sorrow, if your heart ever aches like mine, if you're ever going through hell . . . *then keep going*. Because there's light at the end of every dark tunnel. And it's just a matter of time before you'll bask in it.

An extraordinarily loving friend of mine—who literally forced her way into my house one morning—said those words to me. She convinced me that I needed to change my life and get out of my current rut immediately and *flamboyantly* . . . She persuaded me to say buh-bye to my stinkin' thinkin' and embrace the positive . . . She proved that I needed to lean on friends—like her—to help . . . She made me realize that I needed to love . . . And I needed to spread the love, like a cheerleader . . . Moreover, if I was ever confused about what to do again, I needed to just . . . hug it out. Plain and simple.

Weeks later, when I returned to Seattle Grace, I felt . . . *different*. I stopped thinking about the daunting statistics that the Chief so eloquently pointed out to me on the very first day of my internship. I started thinking more positively. I made friends. *Good* friends. I began talking about my newfound philosophy to anyone who'd listen. And—gosh darn it—on *multiple* occasions, I hugged it out! Before I knew it, I was no longer Sydney "007" Heron. I was now Sydney "heal with love" Heron. My journey—it wasn't nearly over—it was just well underway.

Since then, I've been slowly but surely getting back on track. I've started to think that every smile my mouth forms is a small victory. No, I'll never be able to forget my fatal mistake. The guilt and sorrow—it comes in waves—but it's okay to feel those things once in a while. It only means you're human. It means you're alive and capable of moving on . . .

I realized that, if I were to hold onto the past, then how was I ever supposed to live in the present? That would be impossible, right? I had to accept the fact that, yes, I messed up. Yes, I was going to feel guilty at times. Yes, I was going to feel sad and want to throw up all over my pretty blue scrubs. But, I had to be strong. I had to *forgive myself*. Oh, that's a big one. *Forgiving yourself*. It's one of the hardest things us humans will ever have to do. But, alas, it's just one more step forward in the right direction on our everlasting journey.

So, there you have it. My humble beginnings, if you will. Although yours will be different, the emotions you feel along the way will be the same. I've witnessed the starts of several colleagues' journeys here at SGH. And, I'm always amazed to see my co-workers endure and overcome the same feelings on their own personal voyages. Albeit, in slightly different ways . . .

With Izzie, it was baking and the bathroom floor that helped her through her great depression. I actually had the pleasure of counseling Izzie after the loss of her boyfriend, Denny. You see, it was Izzie who cut Denny's LVAD wire, which ultimately and oh-so-sadly ended up killing him. Even more, Izzie was wearing a prom dress the entire time. Okay, you want details, so here's the quick rundown . . .

Denny was a charming patient in need of a new ticker. The staff simply adored him. He was a frequent guest here—always so positive, charismatic and loving. A true gem! Izzie, in particular, thought the world of him. So much so that the pair actually became engaged! That definitely took their relationship (which was once consisting of intimate games of Scrabble and Izzie-scented sweaters) to an entirely new level. Way before the proposal, however, many of Izzie's peers were beginning to think she was getting way too personally involved with the patient. Yeah, ya think?

Anyway, Denny was growing tired of being constrained to a hospital bed. Indeed, he was a strong, virile man, but was beginning to feel like chopped liver. He had been on the heart donor list for a long, long time. Moreover, Denny's battery-powered heart was yet another source of growing aggravation. You see, Denny was attached to an LVAD machine, a device that was buying him more time as he waited for some good news. But the news seemed to be taking its sweet old time, as both Denny and Izzie became more and more frustrated.

Then, one day, word spread that Denny was to finally receive a new heart! Denny and Izzie were overjoyed! Finally! It seemed that their fairy tale wedding was going to happen after all. Soon, though, their hopes were dashed. Unfortunately, there was *another* patient higher up on the heart recipient list than our Denny. He was going to have to wait a little bit longer . . .

But, not if Izzie had a say in the matter . . .

The LVAD was making Denny's heart almost "too strong." His heart needed to be weaker in order to get ahead of that other patient. So, Izzie devised a plan—one that included cutting Denny's LVAD wire and making sure her fiancé got that heart.

Well, the plan didn't go *exactly* as planned. Denny got his new heart, but he ended up dying after a complication hours later. There was a prom in the hospital earlier that night—so it just so happened that Izzie was wearing a beautiful prom dress as she climbed into the bed of her dead fiancé. It was a sad moment for Seattle Grace. And, it was the beginning of Izzie's own personal journey . . .

Like me, Izzie fell into a deep depression. She felt incredibly guilty, immensely sorrowful and terribly melancholy. She lay on the floor of her bathroom for a full day, wearing her prom dress the whole time. And after Izzie finally mustered the courage to take the dress off, she did nothing but bake . . . Muffin after muffin after muffin . . .

In the wake of his death, Denny left Izzie a check for eight million dollars. Still grief-ridden, Izzie held onto the money. As a matter of fact, I heard she posted the check on her fridge. Like a meaningless piece of paper or a Christmas card that has a picture of someone's unidentified kids on it . . . Eight million dollars wasn't going to bring Denny back . . .

Obviously, Izzie had a severe case of stinkin' thinkin'. It seemed impossible for her to discard the negative and embrace the positive. She was just so angry with herself—something that guilt is almost always able to achieve. At one point, I tried peer counseling her, but I'm not sure how much good I was able to do. I came to realize that Izzie was going to get back on her feet *on her own time*. I suppose that cutting Denny's LVAD wire (while wearing her prom dress) was something Izzie simply *had* to do. No one could've talked her out of it. If she didn't do it—if she never gave Denny that chance—then she would've regretted it for the rest of her life. Sadly, Izzie was doomed either way.

To this day, I'm not entirely sure Izzie has fully recovered. I can see it on her face sometimes: She *still* thinks about Denny.

However, I'm happy to report that, most importantly, Izzie is making *progress*. And she's doing it with—what else—*love*.

Ultimately, Izzie put that eight-million-dollar check to good use. She created a clinic in her former lover's honor. This deed, of course, was created out of *love*. You see, love provides the means to get from point A to point B on your journey. Love makes it easy to see the *good* side of things, instead of the bad. Izzie was able to create something extraordinarily positive out of her situation: a clinic—one that will help thousands of people every year. You, too, can do the same. Well, you may not be able to build an actual clinic, but you will *surely* be able to transform the negative into the positive. And you'll do it with love. It'll be yet another step forward in the right direction on your own personal journey.

Now, whereas Izzie baked muffins and built clinics to deal with her loss, George had sex . . . Lots and lots of sex. Then he got married. I've alluded to this story previously, but I wanted to bring it up one more time. It's another perfect example of how—on their own journeys—people heal with love in *vastly different ways*.

Not too long ago, George's father sadly lost his battle to cancer. It was a devastating moment for George. He was awfully close to his father, Harold. When Harold passed, George began *his* healing journey. One that didn't require George to forgive *himself*, but, rather, his *colleagues* . . .

You see, the doctors needed to operate on Harold to find out exactly how far his cancer had spread. If the disease was too far along, it would compromise Harold's ability to recover from the removal of his cancerous tumor. Doctors would need to close Harold up, and send him home with—unfortunately—a couple of weeks or months to live . . . However, Harold didn't want that. He felt that he was a survivor, a fighter. He wanted the tumor removed regardless of whether the cancer had spread. He didn't want that tumor inside of him any longer, no matter what. Harold told this to the Chief, who attempted to talk Harold out of his decision. The Chief, you see, knew that moving forward with the surgical removal of Harold's tumor was not a good idea if the cancer had spread. But, in the end, it was Harold's decision . . .

So, the doctors opened Harold up and discovered that, yes, the cancer had indeed spread to his other organs. Abiding by Harold's wishes, the surgeons removed the cancerous tumor . . . Harold never survived.

The news crushed George. He *knew* the doctors were well aware that removing Harold's tumor was, in essence, a death sentence. Yet, they proceeded anyway. Oh, if you could've heard George screaming at the Chief and Dr. Bailey. His cries will remain etched in my mind for quite some time.

As a way to cope, George went on a sexual rampage. Sex— lots and lots of sex with Callie. And then, marriage! Yep, George eloped with Callie to Vegas. And, well, you know the rest of *that* story . . .

Clearly, George had a unique way of dealing with his loss: sex. A classic healing with love *newbie*. Sure, George was licking his wounds with love—just *way too much* love. But, you know, George is forgiven because he was just *starting* on his journey. I believe that he, like many of you, will get this whole healing with love thing right, one day. Just keep in mind, what works for George (lots of sex) and Izzie (muffins and clinics) may not work for you. Perhaps, for example, your love will evolve from a higher power. Like Dr. Bailey's does . . .

Very recently, Bailey endured quite an ordeal at the hospital. In a seriously emotional saga, Bailey's baby, Tuck, *almost* lost his life. Oh yes, it was very scary. I've heard rumblings that someone— maybe Bailey, maybe Bailey's husband, maybe someone else—left an important baby gate open at home. Tuck wandered into a room that *should've* been closed off and . . . well . . . a bookshelf tumbled on top of him.

I never saw Bailey so worried and emotional. Boy, did she pray. She prayed to the high heavens! Her first instinct was to blame her husband, but she quickly began to blame herself as well. Yes, *she* may have very well been the one who left that baby gate open. I just hope she doesn't drive herself crazy trying to remember. The good news is, Bailey's baby survived. As for Bailey's marriage, well, *that* may be a different story . . . Hopefully, she won't forget that love heals all . . .

The truth is, we deal with loss, guilt and forgiveness in our own special, unique way. My healing with love principles are simply guidelines. Maybe you need to fire up the oven and start baking muffins instead of saying buh-bye to stinkin' thinkin' at some particular moment. Perhaps you'll opt to become a sex fiend instead of becoming a cheerleader of love (which, I suppose, can be the same thing in some circles). Or, you may very well put your faith in God instead of hugging it out. Here's the thing: As you launch your very own Great Expedition, those choices are really up to you. But, whether you're able to bake, have sex or pray, just remember we all have the ability to love. And that, my friends, is where *all* healing begins.

HERONISM

What's the one thing everybody needs when they decide to embark on a journey? Anybody? Correct—You need a road map! Well, *now* is the time to create your very own "Healing with Love Road Map." This, my friends, will be a very therapeutic exercise. And all you'll need is a pen and paper! How about that?

Begin by thinking back to the beginning of your journey. When did you decide to start healing with love? After a breakup? After the passing of a loved one? After you accidentally left the baby gate open? Whatever the case may be, write your sitch down in the upper left-hand corner of your paper. Now, draw angry little faces or even lightning bolts around your text. This will mark the *beginning* of your journey.

Next, in the lower right-hand corner of your paper, describe how you'd like to feel in a week, a month or even a year. Try to write something positive here. And be as specific as you can. You don't have to write something that relates to the start of your journey, either.

Now, around your text, draw smiley faces, rainbows and whatever else makes you happy. Hey, you can even use different colors here. Make it as bright and lively as you can! This is supposed to be your happy place!

Okay, now begin to draw a line from your dark place (in the upper left-hand corner) to your happy place (in the lower right-hand corner). Go slow! As you're drawing this line, visualize yourself standing in your happy place, basking in the warm glow of sunlight. Think about the steps you're going to take to get there. Reflect on your journey. Think about where you started and, now, where you're headed. Breathe slowly. Breathe deeply. It's important to take as much time as you need to draw this simple straight line.

When you're done, you'll probably notice that you feel excited, energized and rejuvenated. You should feel in control! You should feel *happy!* Good job!

Be sure to keep your map safe. Leave it in a special place. The next time you're feeling a little down, return to your map and draw *another* straight line from start to finish—using the same techniques outlined above. You can come back to your map as often as you'd like. You may even decide to create multiple maps, which is fine by me! Personally, I have about 17 of them.

Remember, your "Healing With Love Road Map" will always be there for you . . . Always ready to keep you calm . . . Always ready to remind you where you're going . . . Always ready to show that sunnier pastures lie right around the corner!

CHAPTER THIRTEEN

Kickass Surgery or Pony Birth?
The Choice Is Yours.

*"In any moment of decision, the best thing you can do is
the right thing, the next best thing is the wrong thing,
and the worst thing you can do is nothing."*
—THEODORE ROOSEVELT

I HAVE A FEELING you're going to be able to get through this next chapter without even breaking a sweat. You're already an old pro at the subject: making decisions. Easy breezy, right? I mean, look at you! Already, you've decided to pick up this book. You've chosen to learn how to heal with love. You've opted to wipe off that mascara, forget about your troubles and embrace the future. You've also been able to successfully answer multiple choice questions as in the following . . . You know what that means! Pop quiz time!

Picture this: You're a first-year surgical intern. Your patient has excessive fluid in his lungs, so your resident tells you to perform a paracentesis (a procedure that will drain the fluid). It'll be your first time attempting such a procedure, but you decide to bite the bullet and go for it. As you drain the fluid from your patient—all of a sudden—he drops dead! What do you do?

A. Panic, cry, scream and then run to the nearest supply closet and hide. Transferring to Mercy West wouldn't be so bad, right?

B. Breathe. Then, find your resident, tell her exactly what happened and prepare for the most brutal tongue-lashing of your life.

C. Can you say, "illegal autopsy"?

Did you make your . . . *decision*? Excellent! The correct answer is "A."

And, "B."

And, "C!"

That's right! *All* three answer choices are indeed correct. (Told ya this chapter would be easy!) The point of that quiz was to get you to make a decision. And, look! You did! No matter what choice you made, the truth of the matter is that you were able to state your problem, think about your options, and decide what to do next. That, my friend, is called making a decision. So, good on you!

Even though all answers were right, your choice tells me a little bit about your personality. If you chose "A," then, even though the thought of making a decision scares the bejesus out of you—even though decisions seem to catapult you into a state of fear, anxiety and utter shock—you're *somehow* able to muster up enough strength to actually make a choice every now and then. You just need some time to think—and you do your best thinking while sitting next to brooms and mops in a supply closet.

If this sounds like you, take solace in the fact that you are not alone, by any means. There are plenty of people out there who are *just like you*. Heck, I even know a few. In fact, I work with a few. The people who don't like change. The people who have a hard time making decisions. The people who are often found hyperventilating in closets. Let me tell you about one of those people in particular. Meredith.

Oh, Meredith and her choices. She's made some pretty bad ones. But, you know, that's the only way she was able to gain experience. And experience was the only way she was able to finally start making some good decisions . . .

Now, from what I've seen, Meredith has been faced with all kinds of choices: getting roommates or living alone, confronting Addison or avoiding her until the end of time, coming back from the dead or remaining in some eerie white void . . . Knitting or sex, tequila or vodka, McDreamy or McVet . . . For the purposes of this chapter, however, let's just focus on that last one . . . A life complete with kickass surgeries and Derek—*or*—one full of pony births and the neighborhood veterinarian, Finn. Decisions, decisions . . .

Meredith met Finn back when she was on her celibacy kick. She had vowed that, instead of sex, she would *knit*. Well—as soon as she picked up her needles, Meredith met Finn—the handsome veterinarian who seemed to put her celibacy declaration on pause. Finn was a doll. He came by the hospital a few times to give Meredith updates on her sick dog, Doc. The poor fella. Not Finn. Doc. The dog. Anyhoo—Derek was still making a go at it with Addison, so Meredith started seeing Finn and . . . well . . . McVet was born.

And then the Prom happened, which just threw a wrench into *everybody's* plans. The interns were forced to blow up a whole slew of balloons, Burke realized his hand tremor was there to stay, Izzie lost Denny, Bailey and the Chief contemplated what to do about LVAD wire-cutting interns, *I* got sick off of way-too-spiked punch and . . . Meredith slept with

Derek. Talk about a night to remember! Was that our prom theme? Well, it should've been . . .

So, where was I? Oh, yes, Meredith and Derek sleeping together, behind their dates' backs, in a patient room, at the prom. When Addison found that pair of black panties in Derek's tuxedo pocket, well, she knew *exactly* who they belonged to.

The deal was done. Yes, Addison and Derek were over. And so, Meredith was left with a choice: Continue to see Finn or rekindle her romance with the now available Derek?

Like I said, Meredith isn't the biggest fan of making decisions. Finn or Derek? McDreamy or McVet? Surgeries or pony births? The trailer or the vet's office? Oh, a closet to hyperventilate in was *just* around the corner . . . A decision was too hard to reach so . . . Meredith didn't make one. Instead, she decided to date (i.e., she decided to stall).

Good for her, I say. Quick decisions aren't always the best, you know. Surprisingly enough, Meredith—having learned from her mistakes, after hiding in one too many supply closets, after being so concerned about change—actually decided (for once) to take her time making a decision.

Mer evaluated her prospects: Derek had professed his love to her. Finn had brought her lunch. Derek invited her to scrub in on an awesome surgery. Finn had ice cream. Oh, boy, the decision was getting harder and harder for Meredith to make . . .

It only took a little bit of morphine to finally knock some sense and resolve into Meredith. While recovering from that appendicitis I told you all about, Meredith chose . . . drum roll please . . . Derek! (As if you didn't already know.)

It wasn't easy for her, but Meredith was able to move forward and make her choice. I suppose that indecision always turns into decision with time. I really am glad that Meredith took her time with this one, though. In the past, she's been so disturbed by the idea of making a decision that she either a) acts rashly and impulsively, or b) refuses to decide altogether. Neither of those options were good for her. With choice "a," Meredith either ended up with her hand stuck on a bomb in a body cavity or in bed with some stranger she picked up at Joe's. And, she never got anywhere except that dirty, old supply closet when she went with choice "b." Obviously, Meredith was trying to learn from all of those things when deciding to take her time and date as a way of deciding between her two suitors. It was experience! And, like I said, experience leads to good decision-making. Mer's still not a perfect decider, but she'll get there . . . one day . . . eventually . . . *hopefully*.

Now, if you selected "B" in this chapter's pop quiz, then you, my friend, are where Meredith and many, many wishy-washy people *want* to be! You're the cautious type by nature and you probably already make good decisions. That's because you like to do everything by the book. You really think about all of your options before you go ahead and make a decision. You may even pull out a notebook so that you can list the pros vs. the cons of each choice! You're the person who actually takes a moment to collect your thoughts, gather as much information as you can and *evaluate*. Luckily, you're usually fortunate enough to have a clear head to do so.

When you don't have a clear head to make a decision, it's sometimes necessary to just get away from it all. Never be afraid to, say, go on a camping trip with your friends. The peace and quiet will rejuvenate you, clear your mind, and allow you to make a good, solid decision.

It was crucial for Derek, for instance, to go on a camping expedition with the boys when Meredith told him that she broke up with Finn. Derek, you see, truly loved Meredith. He sensed that Meredith's decision between her two suitors was torturing her. It was only bringing her pain. So, McDreamy being McDreamy went to Meredith and told her that he was backing out of the competition. He didn't want to bring Meredith any more pain. He had accepted the fact that no, he may not win back the love of his life. So, it came as quite a shock when Meredith just blurted out that she had broken up with Finn (and, in effect, chosen Derek). That was some pretty big news, right?

Well, Derek needed some time of his own to contemplate Meredith's decision before he could go any further. Thus, he went camping with his comrades in order to get a little personal thinking done. When Derek returned, he decided to "take it slow" with Meredith. And a well-informed, good decision was made!

The Chief, you know, was another person to benefit from the boys' venture into the woods. Yes, he accompanied Derek, Burke, George, Alex, Joe the bartender and his boyfriend, Walter, on— from what I hear—quite an eventful trip. How those boys got *any* thinking done is beyond me! Slap fights, hand tremor discoveries, a MacGyver surgery—with all of that drama going on, it's hard to picture Derek and Richard taking some "me" time to reflect on their woes.

Prior to the trip, Richard had quite the choice to make: his wife Adele, or his hospital. Adele, you see, gave her husband that ultimatum. She was sick and tired of Richard always seeming to give the hospital priority over her. I heard that things got so bad between the two that Adele kicked Richard out! Yes, it seemed that Richard was holed up at the Archfield Hotel, a popular destination among the staff at Seattle Grace.

Well, Richard was certainly feeling the heat. One day, I remember, he came in asking for help sewing a button onto his shirt. The man was down to his last clean shirt! The poor Chief. Aw, he was so frustrated, pleading for either a good dry cleaner or a good tailor. Adele, he said, used to handle his buttons. It was quite a sight, let me tell you!

Clearly, the Chief, like most doctors, is a *cautious* decision maker. He needed time to think about what to do about his wife . . . and his job. He ultimately decided to retire and finally step down as Chief, but when he finally went to tell Adele . . . it seemed he was too late. Adele had already moved on. Lesson learned: It's okay to take time to evaluate your options, but, like everything, there *is* a time limit. It's a balance. You can't take forever to make a decision. But, you can't be too quick either . . .

Which brings me to answer "C" on our beloved pop quiz. If you picked that choice, then watch out! You, my sassy dear, are always ready to throw caution to the wind and act on a decision as soon as one needs to be made. You're adventurous. You laugh in the face of danger. However, you often get yourself into some rather sticky situations, right? Yes, because of your impulsive nature, you sometimes get caught between a rock and a hard place. Even so, you believe the excitement gained from leaping without always looking is well worth any and all risk!

Cristina and Izzie are classic choosers of answer "C." Cristina, well, she's pretty fearless. And, Izzie? Well, you know how that LVAD-wire story goes. As a matter of fact, it was Cristina and Izzie who performed an illegal autopsy on the paracentesis guy from our pop quiz. Yes, the two of them made the rash decision (without prior consent) to go ahead and find out *exactly* what went wrong during their procedure. And, when Bailey discovered what they were up to . . . Well, have you ever seen someone so angry you can literally see the lasers shooting from her eyes and the smoke emanating from her ears? Well, that was Dr. Bailey!

Cristina and Izzie clearly didn't take their own little camping trip to consider the pros and cons of their decision now, did they? In the end, however, Cristina and Izzie's choice turned out to be a good one. They ended up learning that their patient died—not because of any negligence—but because of a previously unknown genetic condition. The same genetic condition that could have affected their patient's daughter. And, because Cristina and Izzie discovered all of this, they ended up potentially saving that woman's own life. So, it looks as though even if you're an adventurous decision maker, you're *still* capable of making the *right* decision. As I said, it doesn't matter which answer choice you chose in that little pop quiz of mine, it just matters that you actually chose.

Now, if you were *not* able to pick an answer in the quiz, then you must be in *a lot* of pain. Am I right? Tell me, how does inside reader feel right now? Not very good, I bet! You're indecisive, which can be torturous. The truth is, the risk you take by making a *wrong* decision is better than indecision. Not being able to decide on something is a horrendous, frustrating feeling. Decisions, you see, allow you to be happy. The next time you make a decision, about anything, stop for a moment and reflect on how you feel at that exact moment. I guarantee you—peace, serenity, joy, fulfillment—you'll have the pleasure of feeling it all.

In case you're wondering, I'm the type of gal who would choose "B" on our little pop quiz. I'll admit it—I'm safe. That pros vs. cons thing? Guilty! Right here! It's something yours truly does every time I need to make a decision. For example, remember the leg that was being eaten alive by flesh-eating bacteria? Not so pretty, I know. Well, while working with Cristina and Alex on that case, I needed to choose whether to attempt to save my patient's leg or amputate (Cristina's choice). As you know, I opted to save that poor girl's leg. And, you can bet your sweet bippy that I had my trusty pros vs. cons list to guide me! Yes, I evaluated the situation, studied my options, listed the repercussions of each and . . . *made a decision*.

The simple fact is, making a decision is a healthy thing to do.

After all, life is just the summation of one choice after another. So, if you're choosin', you're livin'. And—as always—if you're livin', you're lovin'. An obvious correlation. The choices you make should *always* reflect the love in your heart. That being said, making right decisions allows you to move forward . . .

I'm certain that there's one decision every single one of us can, and should, make. And, that is *to love*. If you fail to make *that* decision—what's left? Loneliness? Loss? Despair? Sorrow? Now that doesn't sound too appetizing, does it? So, the choice is yours—what's it going to be?

CHAPTER FOURTEEN

I Can Build a Clinic Too!

"Taste the relish to be found in competition—
in having put forth the best within you."

—HENRY J. KAISER,
industrialist

I T'S CERTAINLY A dog-eat-dog world out there, isn't it?
Think about it. Long days. Longer nights. Going above and
beyond the call of duty every single time you set foot in this
hospital. Working your little tush off for the Chief, just hoping—
praying—that he'll someday recognize your natural abilities and
realize that those other lickspittles pale in comparison. Then, the
day comes. The day that all your hard work is *supposed* to pay off.
But, does it? No. Because *Callie* is named Chief Resident. Callie!
Why? Why, I ask. Whhhyyyy??!! What'd I tell ya? Dog-eat-dog.

That's a true story. Shocker, right? Well, clearly, the best
woman (or man) doesn't *always* win. Yes, Mother used to warn
me that competition can *sometimes* get ugly. Well, boy was she
right! Competition sure has a habit of rearing its ugly little head
around Seattle Grace every now and then. From hot-dog-eating
contests to the race for Chief Resident to all of our attendings
jockeying for the Chief of Surgery position, SGH certainly has
a boatload of cutthroat, bloodthirsty competitors roaming its
halls.

It's important to remember that competition is *supposed* to bring out the best in people. Sure, it doesn't always work that way, but that, my friends, is the intention. You're going to have to fight in order to get what you want. And you're going to have to fight fairly. That means strengthening your skills, highlighting your abilities and trying your *best*. And, I suppose, if building a clinic or shuffling paperwork for the Chief is your best, then, so be it . . .

Ah, the race for Chief Resident. It's not just a fancy title, you know. It's actually a *very* big job. The supervising, the managing, the scheduling . . . Sure, it's a lot of work, but the respect you gain from your bosses and peers makes it all worthwhile. The race for this highly coveted position was a close one. Callie, Bailey and myself were the frontrunners for quite some time. We were all pretty unique competitors. Bailey had her clinic. Callie had her paperwork. And I had my cheerful attitude (which I believe mattered the most).

I was absolutely certain I was going to win. And that wasn't just me being Miss Positive Thinker! The Chief just seemed so encouraging. He was always smiling at me. Always "requesting" me. I could tell I had a special place in his heart. Which is why I was so surprised to see Callie's name up on that bulletin board. Chief Resident Callie? Seriously?

You know, to be honest, if the job wasn't going to go to me, then I expected that it would go to Bailey. But Callie? Never in a million years would I have chosen the ortho doc who seemed to take breaking bones a little seriously for the Chief Resident position. I mean, Bailey had built a clinic! That must've looked good on her résumé, don't you think?

That clinic—it really is something. Eight million dollars worth of something! On one hand, I was glad Izzie was able to honor Denny with the clinic. However, on the other hand, I was a bit taken aback when Bailey was able to use the clinic for her own personal gain! Oh, sure, she'll never admit it, but Bailey, my friends, was using that clinic as a power play for the Chief Resident job. The clinic—it saved lives. It helped the underprivileged. It expanded the hospital's clientele. It served as a shrine to Denny. And, now, it was supposed to get Bailey the job. My, my, my . . . People around here sure do play dirty, don't they?

"Go ahead, Dr. Bailey, start a clinic," I thought. "Who cares?" A clinic wasn't going to get her anywhere. Chief Resident is about patient care, not big think, so a big ol' clinic wasn't going to do Bailey any good. I dismissed her efforts. For about a day. And, then, I started noticing that the Chief was actually impressed with Bailey. After all, the clinic was turning into a successful endeavor. It was growing by the day, as a matter of fact. And the Chief was delighted. That's when I wanted to tell him . . . Well, Chief . . . I can build a clinic, too!

Here, we have the ugly side of competition. You see, the race put me in a rut. A self-comparing, self-defeating, envious rut. And, I'm telling you, it *crippled* me. But, sometimes, that's just what competition does . . . You start comparing yourself to your competitors. You start thinking that you've been defeated even before the race has come to an end. You start feeling jealous. It's a horrible position to be in, but, luckily, with the healing power of love on your side, you can *easily* get yourself out of it!

First of all, comparing yourself to others goes against one of the basic principles of my healing with love philosophy. That is, loving yourself. You have to love *yourself*, and, in order to do so, you have to count *your* blessings—*not* your competitors. Basic as that principle may be, it's not so simple. Take it from yours truly! Back when I would saunter through the clinic, closely examining every shiny nook and cranny, I wasn't counting my blessings. I was counting Dr. Bailey's. I might've dismissed the relevance of the clinic publicly, but, that was just *outside* Sydney talking. *Inside* Sydney, meanwhile, was telling an entirely different story.

You see, comparing yourself to others just makes you bitter. You begin to focus on everything your competition has, and fail to recognize the reality of what you yourself have to offer. You start to lose sight of your own abilities and—pretty soon—you forget about them entirely. You begin to doubt yourself. You begin to feel worthless. You begin to feel *defeated* and the Chief hasn't even picked the winner yet! You don't think you're going to win, and that's when you become jealous. You've gone to your dark, desolate, decrepit place. You're *certainly* not loving yourself at that point!

It's a vicious cycle. A dangerous road to follow. And, it's all *a waste of time*. Look, you spent an entire day worried about the clinic and, more importantly, what the Chief thought about the clinic. I think we all know that you could've been a bit more productive with your time! Remember, it's about being your *best*. Is your best comparing the number of patients you treated to the number of patients Bailey treated that day? Is your best eavesdropping on the Chief to hear him talk about "the amazing clinic that Dr. Bailey is doing an excellent job of getting off the ground"? Is your best sitting in the residents' lounge, contemplating how in the world you're going to build a bigger and better clinic all by yourself? I don't think so!

You could've been treating patients of your own, scrubbing in, saving lives, complimenting the Chief on his new darker 'do . . . You know, the stuff that would've actually made a difference and gotten you the job! But, you didn't. Instead of recognizing your own unique talents and *loving yourself*, you got caught up in the unimportant business of others. And, as a result, you watched someone else take the prize.

At that point, when the Chief named Callie our Chief

Resident, I must admit that I felt terribly sad. I was defeated. But, it was something I just had to accept. Trust me, at some point, defeat will be something *you'll* have to just accept as well. And that's precisely when you must—you *absolutely must*—stay positive. You must remember that everything happens for a reason. My defeat, for example, allowed me to rediscover my ardent passion for the OR. I realized that *that's* where I belong. Juggling schedules, managing reports, filling out mounds and mounds of paperwork . . . That's really what being Chief Resident means. Of course, I didn't know that when I began vying for the job, but, when I didn't get it . . . I actually counted my blessings. Hey, I had all the OR time in the world. I got to go home at a decent hour every now and then. I wasn't as stressed out all the time. As for Callie, well, she certainly didn't seem to be reaping *any* of those benefits . . .

Around the time Callie was named Chief Resident, her husband's indiscretions were beginning to come to light. Yes, Callie was definitely dealing with a whole lot of family strife as she struggled to fulfill the duties of her new job. In short, the position was kickin' her little booty. Moreover, it was painfully obvious to Callie: George and Izzie were having an affair. Well, in reality, they only slept together once, but, somehow, Callie knew *something* was up.

George tried to tell Callie about his one night stand with Izzie, but Callie wouldn't let him. Literally! Rumor has it that George was about to lay it all out on the table when Callie pleaded for him to remain silent. She just didn't want to deal with it on top of her new demanding job. Eventually, though, George managed to tell Callie *everything*.

So, it looked like Callie was headed for divorce, and her job wasn't getting much easier . . . Her responsibilities soon fell by the wayside. She started ignoring her paperwork and actually began to hide from the job in the OR. Callie simply couldn't handle it. So, she relied on Bailey to pick up her slack. Well, let me tell you, Bailey *certainly* rose to the occasion!

Bailey had already told Callie that she'd be her number two. And, what do you know, Bailey soon became number one, because as soon as the Chief realized *she* was the best person for that job (and that she had *always* been), Bailey replaced Callie as Chief Resident.

Callie, of course, was a brave little soldier. She didn't seem to be upset at all. In fact, she actually told me she was happy for Bailey. Yes, after getting fired, it seemed that Callie was *finally* healing with love. She started counting her blessings! And, clearly, the Chief Resident job was *not* a blessing to be counted. That position was just making her feel like a failure. So, in a way, Callie losing her job was a blessing in disguise. It used to be hard for Callie to love herself after her long, arduous days as Chief Resident. Today, however, Callie seems so much happier. She doesn't have to worry about schedules and paperwork. All she has to worry about is *herself*. You see, that's *exactly* what the amazing healing power of love can do: turn any self-defeat into a self-win.

You know, Chief Resident is just a small potato when you think about the larger picture here. At Seattle Grace, there's an even *bigger* race to be won. I know, can you believe it? I'm talking about the race for Chief of Surgery. When Richard announced he was stepping down, all of our attendings were thrown into a tizzy. Oh yeah, this contest is for the big boys, people. Actually, it's one for the big boys and one big, red-headed girl . . .

From the very beginning, even before the Chief made his official announcement, it was *Burke* who thought he had the job in the bag. Burke always believed he was SGH's top surgeon, so he was a bit stunned when—one day—*Derek* showed up. You see, Richard brought Derek to Seattle specifically to compete for the

Chief position. He felt that Burke had gotten too complacent, too comfortable. So, in an effort to keep Burke on his toes—and bring out the very best in everyone—Richard hired his old friend Derek, who happened to be Manhattan's finest neurosurgeon. Well, ding-a-ding-ding! The fight had begun with Derek and Burke in the ring!

The two attendings duked it out for quite some time. But, when Richard needed an eye operation, he named Burke as interim Chief. Clearly, it was a blow to Derek's ego. Furthermore, the Chief's decision coincided with his discovery of Derek and Meredith's relationship. Richard didn't exactly approve of his alleged "star attending" sleeping with an intern. Even though Richard told Derek that his choice was "nothing personal," Derek couldn't help but think his relationship with Meredith was, indeed, a factor.

Around that same time, *Addison* arrived at Seattle Grace. Richard had called on her skills for a high-profile, neonatal case. And, well, who better to have around than one of the world's foremost neonatal surgeons, right? Richard had known both Addison and Derek from his days in New York, so it was a reunion of some sort. Of course, Derek was definitely *not* happy that Richard summoned Addison to SGH. "Nothing personal?" *Oh, really?*

Along with many, many pairs of gorgeous shoes, Addison also brought divorce papers to Seattle as well. Addison told Derek that if he signed the papers, she'd be on the first plane back to Manhattan. The choice was his. Well, Derek mulled the decision over and—in the end—*did not* sign the divorce papers. Meredith, of course, was appalled . . .

Addison was there to stay. And she planned to compete for the Chief of Surgery job as well. Hey, she was getting her life back together and making a real go at it with Derek. Why not compete with the boys for the fancy office, too? After all, she had everything they had, and then some. Of course, as you know, Addison and Derek didn't work out . . . They ultimately divorced and Derek returned to Meredith.

A fourth competitor later entered the race . . . *Mark*. That's right—Mark the manwhore. Hey, just because he's a manwhore doesn't mean he'd make a bad Chief of Surgery. Right? Well, I don't know about that one . . .

Yes—Burke, Derek, Addison and Mark. *One* of them was going to be our next Chief. But who? Richard finally announced that he was planning to retire *that year*—and, that's when the competition *really* heated up. And, of course, that's when things got ugly.

The attendings started showing off. One-upping each other. It got messy. So, the Chief brought in a ringer . . . *Colin Marlowe*. *The* Colin Marlowe. The Colin Marlowe who was both a cardiothoracic legend *and* Cristina's ex-boyfriend. Boy, I'm telling you, never a dull moment at Seattle Grace!

With the other attendings caught up in their childish, playground-like, "my scrub cap is better than yours" antics, it looked like Dr. Marlowe was the frontrunner for a period of time. However, it turned out that Dr. Marlowe wasn't actually there for the job . . . Nope. He was there for Cristina. You see, he was still in love with her. Alas, Cristina told the living legend that her feelings for him subsided a long time ago. Soon after, Marlowe left Seattle Grace . . .

All of this prompted the attendings to realize that they needed to tweak their strategies and go in for the kill. So, Burke worked on his confidence and tried his hardest to keep his head in the game. He had a lot going on, you know. Burke always believed that people looked at him differently after his hand tremor debacle. Would his peers ever respect him as Chief? On top of that, Dr. Marlowe had been there trying to steal Cristina, which seemed to open up a *huge* can of worms. What, did Cristina collect famous cardiothoracic surgeons like baseball cards? Is she really capable of marriage? Or, will she just leave—like she did with Marlowe—when she's done learning from a mentor? With all of these questions and doubts running through his mind, Burke fought to remain focused. It seemed like Burke really could've benefited from a friend or two. But, where was he going to find one of those? All of his "friends" seemed to be his competition. Oh, poor Burke.

Derek, on the other hand, decided to back off on his relationship with Meredith. He noticed that it was affecting his chances of getting the Chief's job. You see, when Ellis died, Derek realized that Richard felt an obligation to protect Meredith. Richard started looking after Meredith and making sure she had everything she needed. And, what Meredith needed most was security. But Richard knew that the Chief of Surgery job didn't exactly breed security for loved ones. He knew that from experience. As Chief, you're never home, you neglect your family and you miss out on important things. Clearly, Richard wouldn't want Meredith to have to deal with a partner who's never there. Richard told Derek that's *exactly* what Meredith would have to deal with if he were to be named the next Chief of Surgery . . . So Derek backed off. Now that I think of it, Derek could've benefited from having a true friend around during that time, too.

As for Mark's strategy, well . . . he used his own innate, natural talents to impress the Chief . . . He introduced Richard to "the ladies." See, Mark believed that some good, old-fashioned male bonding would secure his place as Seattle Grace's next Chief of Surgery. So, he became Richard's "wingman." They went to Joe's, where Mark proceeded to teach the Chief about "women." It was certainly a sight to behold. Poor Richard. He was just a little out of practice, that's all. Personally, I think the Chief is quite a catch. But, that's neither here nor there . . . Anyhoo! It looked like Mark had actually found a friend—the most important friend to have when it came to the race for Chief. But, was it going to be enough for Mark to win?

And, finally, there was Addison. Her strategy was simple . . . Let the boys destroy one another and be the only woman left standing. It was a good one. Unfortunately, it didn't work. Maybe because she didn't tweak or change her strategy when it was necessary.

The Chief eventually made his decision. Our new Chief of Surgery was going to be . . . Derek! I suppose Derek's strategy to let go of Meredith (just a little) worked because it looked like he was going to be our next Chief.

Again, however, the best woman (or man) doesn't always win. *At first*, that is. Yes, rumors abound that when Derek was named Chief, he told Richard that he couldn't take the job. He wasn't the best man. Instead, *Richard* remained the best man. Derek, you see, wanted Richard to do it all over again. To learn from his mistakes. To give it another shot. To do things *differently*. Well, I couldn't agree more: Richard and *only Richard* is the best person for the Chief of Surgery job.

Well, it seems that all of our attendings fought the good fight, wouldn't you agree? At the end of the day, I suppose competition leaves you with two options. One, you can lose. Or, two, you can change *and win*. That's certainly what I've learned. That's certainly what Bailey, Callie and our attendings have learned. Moreover, that's absolutely what Richard learned. He decided to make the biggest change of all—to do things *differently*. It's an honest thing to do. I truly hope he succeeds.

The thing I love about competition is that it has the ability to bring out the best in you. As long as you avoid its ugly side—the comparison, the doubting, the defeating, the jealousy—competition is actually healthy. The truth is—you're not going to be able to win every contest. There's always someone else that's going to be able to eat more hot dogs than you. So, when you do lose, don't forget to look on the bright side of things. You're not the one who's going to taste hot dog all afternoon. You're not the one who's going to be sick in an hour. You're not the one who's going to drown in a sea of paperwork. You're not the one who's going to have the responsibility of running a multi-million-dollar, cutting-edge hospital surgical wing. In every situation of defeat, remember, there's always going to be at least one blessing to count . . . No competition will ever be able to defeat your *ability to love*. And, *that's* certainly worth counting—right?

HERONISM

It takes a clear mind and a positive attitude to win any competition. You *have* to remain focused and you *have* to keep your eyes on the prize. Moreover, you *have* to tune all of those negative thoughts and complaints out of your mind. Here's a simple technique that will enable you to do so: Create a Sydney-Zone!

A Sydney-Zone is a designated area where gossip cannot be spread and complaints cannot be uttered. While standing in (or passing through) a Sydney-Zone, you (and those around you) will not be able to mutter a single negative phrase. Self-comparison? There's definitely no room for *that* in a Sydney-Zone. Jealousy? No way, Jose! Feelings of defeat? Forget about it!

Instead, think about your accomplishments while visiting a Sydney-Zone. Talk about your goals, dreams and aspirations.

Compliment your friends. Remain committed to encouragement and optimism. A Sydney-Zone is chock full of positive
energy!

To designate your very own Sydney-Zone, I've found that
yellow police tape works extremely well. You can even try
putting red tape on the ground, outlining the borders of your
zone. A Sydney-Zone can be as big or as small as you'd like.
Of course, be sure to get permission from your boss if you
decide to create a Sydney-Zone at work. Enjoy!

CHAPTER FIFTEEN

To Follow or Not to Follow . . .
in Mommy's Footsteps

"Children begin by loving their parents. As they grow older,
they judge them. Sometimes, they forgive them."

—OSCAR WILDE

HERE'S SOMETHING YOU probably didn't know about me: *I* was a wild child. Sad, but true! In elementary school—when everybody else was drawing smiley faces in art class—*I* was doodling short, fat and bald Mr. McGillis. He never even had a clue—the poor fella.

In seventh grade, I absolutely refused to wrap my books. You remember wrapping your books, right? It was a requirement at Captain James E. Daly Junior High. In order to protect those sacred textbooks, I was *supposed* to wrap their covers in paper and draw colorful little stars on them. Well, this idea of book-wrapping just sent me over the edge! Think about all of that paper being wasted! So, I refused. And, my teachers were *not* pleased.

In high school—that's when I seemed to turn *really* bad. I would go to the public library and stay there *all night*. Yep—even till nine o'clock on some Saturday evenings! Boy oh boy, I was a real lean mean teen, let me tell you.

I recall—one night—spending a good six hours at the library

with my nose firmly planted in a novel that was supposed to be read by college-aged students. Well, I must've lost track of time, because before I knew it—the library was closing! I checked my digital watch, which read: 8:47 p.m. My stomach dropped! I was supposed to be home for dinner! I ran up to the front desk, checked the novel out and booked it outta there. My feet couldn't carry me fast enough! I *tried* quietly sneaking in the house, but as soon as I opened the door—sure enough—there stood my mother, drinking her nightly cup of tea. She caught me, red-handed. I was totally late and—even worse—I was holding a college-level book.

"Oh, Syd," Mother said. "What are we going to do with you?"

Then, she went right back to enjoying her tea.

I'm actually quite surprised that I never ended up serving a lengthy sentence in solitary confinement at the juvenile detention center just across the river. Luckily, my parents took a different approach to discipline . . . One that Mr. and Mrs. Heron called *encouragement*.

You see, when I brought home that drawing of Mr. McGillis, my parents smiled and bought me art supplies. When teachers called to complain about my stance on the book-wrapping trade, my parents laughed and sided with *me*. And, when my parents noticed my interest in advanced reading-level books, they introduced me to even *more* of them. They praised my natural talents and abilities. They applauded what they called "my strong sense-of-self." They told me to "always stand up for what I believe in." They *encouraged*. Moreover, they *loved*.

Well, I guess it worked! Because I didn't turn out so bad, now, did I? What's funny is that I seemed to have turned out just like *them*. My parents! Indeed, I seemed to have inherited my father's confidence. Likewise, I seemed to have acquired my mother's penchant for a nightly cup of tea. Right down to the teaspoon of honey and half-second pour of skim milk! Of course, I also seem to have retained both Mom and Dad's philosophy of encouragement mixed with a little bit of pure, unfiltered love.

When, exactly, did I turn into my parents? Well, I'll tell ya . . . It was when I *decided* to!

That's right, it was *my decision*. I chose to encourage. I chose to love. I chose to have that steaming hot cup of lavender tea right before I retired to bed last night. And, I'll *continue* to do it because I *want* to do it. Look, I don't preach encouragement and love—or drink tea—because that's what my parents believed in. I preach encouragement and love because it's what I, Sydney Heron, believe in.

So, I have a nightly tea vice. Big deal! I can't blame my mother just because she had one too. Likewise, if I had . . . say . . . oh, I don't know . . . a sleeping-with-inappropriate-men vice . . . then, I wouldn't blame my mother if she dealt with the same demons, too. Are you following me?

Your vices, your problems, your hangups, your actions—they are all *your own*. Your mother and father cannot be blamed. It is you—and only you—who's in control of your own destiny. No matter what, it's important for *you* to take responsibility.

I'm lucky. My parents were always there for me—ready to help me with my homework, ready to tell me the definition of a word I didn't know, ready to tell me the correct way to draw a short, fat art teacher's bald spot. Some of you aren't as fortunate. You may have a father who's completely out of the picture. Maybe he's a drunk who was never able to stand up to your mother. Or, perhaps, you have a mother who's unable to devote any time to you because of her job, or because of her love affair with a man at her job. Whatever the case may be, *now* is the time to declare that you are your own person! That is the first crucial step to healing after having moms and dads like the ones I just mentioned.

Keep in mind, if you had parents who seemed to let you down rather than bring you up, you're not alone. Trust me, many people have had unhappy childhoods. Just remember, it's not a requirement to follow in your mom or dad's footsteps. It's simply a *choice* . . .

As the daughter of a world-famous surgeon, you'd think that Meredith—of all people—would have it a little more together, right? Well, she doesn't! Meredith, you see, is one of those people who had a bit of a troubled childhood. For one thing, her mother was *never* home. Ellis was married to her job. So, she spent days on end at the hospital. As for Meredith's father, Thatcher, well, he wasn't around all that much either. Why? I already told you, silly! Because Ellis was married to her job . . . Which eventually caused Ellis to start having an affair with a co-worker, which ultimately caused Ellis and Thatcher's marriage to suffer, which then made Thatcher start drinking, which, in the end, made Thatcher leave. That's right, Thatcher left Ellis and—in doing so—left Meredith as well.

And, voilà, Meredith's so-called abandonment issue was born.

As you know, the co-worker that Ellis began seeing turned out to be Richard, who is now both my and Meredith's boss. Ellis and Richard had a whirlwind of a romance. They quickly fell in love and planned to leave their spouses. Well, Ellis at least kept *her* end of the deal. Yes, Thatcher was officially out of the picture. But, when push came to shove around a beautiful, spinning carousel—Richard told Ellis that he just wasn't able to keep his word and leave Adele. So went the end of Richard and Ellis' affair . . .

Sadly, Meredith was an innocent witness to *all* of her mother's indiscretions. You see, five-year-old Meredith was on that spinning carousel, watching Richard and Ellis end their relationship.

That's not something you just conveniently forget, you know. Then, years later, the older Meredith was forced to hear about the details of the affair while caring for her Alzheimer's-afflicted mother who seemed to be re-living it. Yes, Meredith (and much of the hospital) learned all about Ellis' broken marriage every time the esteemed surgeon paid a visit to Seattle Grace. It was *not* a pretty sight.

As for Thatcher, he remarried a wonderful woman named Susan. When Ellis passed, it was Susan who became Meredith's "fake mom." Susan visited Meredith at work, checked up on her and even invited her over for dinner . . . One morning, Meredith woke up and found Susan in her kitchen, unloading groceries into her fridge! Yes, Meredith was definitely not used to *that* kind of attention, especially from a mother-figure. She had dealt with overbearing, but, as for overprotective? That was a whole new experience.

Of course, along with Susan came the resurfacing of Thatcher. All of a sudden, Meredith was seeing more and more of her once long-lost father. They were actually forming a bit of a relationship. Thatcher was even able to fix Meredith's porch swing! Yes this was certainly all new for Meredith. Her familial relationships were finally seeming to get back on track . . . That is, until Susan died.

It wasn't supposed to be a big deal. Susan came into the clinic with some pretty persistent hiccups. So Dr. Bailey gave her a drug which seemed to stop them, but only temporarily. When Susan returned, still hiccupping, the doctors decided to do an outpatient procedure that would finally put an end to Susan's dilemma. However, the ensuing surgery seemed to cause a complication—Susan came back to SGH with a small heart murmur. She was given antibiotics, which helped for a moment, but ultimately led to an even bigger, more serious (and rare) problem: toxic megacolon with a perforation. Susan was septic! She was rushed to an OR, where Meredith and a team of doctors did everything they could . . . Sadly, however, Susan didn't survive . . .

Meredith had to tell Thatcher the disturbing news. But, what turned out to be perhaps even more disturbing was Thatcher's reaction . . . He slapped Meredith across the face. In front of the Chief. In front of Derek. In front of the entire hospital.

Obviously, Meredith and Thatcher's relationship became quite strained after that debacle. Thatcher actually returned to drinking. On the day of Susan's funeral, as a matter of fact, he showed up at the hospital, completely drunk. Thatcher told Meredith he didn't want to see her at the funeral. It was a *horrible* scene to witness. As a result, Meredith and Thatcher's relationship remains severely awkward to this day. And—even more distressing—Thatcher continues to battle his addiction to alcohol.

Now, as if all of that family drama weren't enough for Meredith to handle, she currently has to *work* with Lexie, Thatcher and Susan's daughter. Or, as Derek once had the nerve to call her: "The girl from the bar." That's right—Derek and Lexie met at Joe's Bar, the night before Lexie's first day as an intern. Sound familiar? It should—because that's exactly how Derek and Meredith met. Yes, Lexie was, in fact, the *other* girl from the bar. Poor Meredith. Talk about *awkward!*

In the beginning, Meredith despised Lexie. I mean, from Mer's point of view, here was this chick who called herself "the girl from the bar" and claimed to be Meredith's "sister." Oh, yes she did! Lexie basically stalked Meredith for quite some time. She simply "wanted to get to know her." But, Meredith wasn't having any of that. Lexie, you see, was *not* a girl that Meredith wanted to get to know . . .

As far as Mer was concerned, she absolutely *did not* have a sister. Moreover, when Lexie insinuated that she and Mer had the same father, well, Meredith saw red . . . According to Meredith, her dad was *so* not the same as Lexie's. Meredith's dad disappeared when she was five and never bothered to call her again. Does that sound like the same father that Lexie knew? Meredith didn't think so . . .

Over time, however, Meredith couldn't help but get to know Lexie. Indeed, she made a very touching attempt toward—I suppose—what you could call "a relationship." One evening, Meredith read Susan's death note to Lexie. She outlined every single thing that happened on the tragic night Susan lost her life. It was emotional, but it needed to be done—for the sake of both Meredith *and* Lexie.

Despite all the awkwardness, it looked like the two long-lost "sisters" were finally headed toward a wonderfully beautiful relationship. That is, until Lexie decided to sleep with Alex. In Meredith's house. Uh-oh! Well, it was just way too much for Mer to take—now Lexie was sleeping with her friends? Seriously? Heck, no! But, in an attempt to patch things over, Lexie told Meredith five things about herself. You see, Lexie figured that those five things would make it a little more difficult for Meredith to hate her. Well, it seemed to work . . . Taken aback by Lexie's forwardness (and the fact that Lexie plays the trombone), Meredith actually allowed Alex to take her home from the bar that night . . .

Well, it has certainly been a rocky road for Meredith and Lexie. But, I'm happy to say that they now seem to be on the right path. Recently, Meredith even cooked breakfast for Lexie! Eggs! Now, considering Meredith *does not* cook—anything—I'd say this breakfast for champions was a giant step in a positive direction. What's funny is that Lexie is actually allergic to eggs. Yet, being the child of an adult alcoholic, Lexie *had* to eat them. Boundary issues, she said. Lexie's severe boundary issues weren't going to let her refuse Meredith's eggs . . .

Which brings me back to the message I want to get across in this chapter . . . Your issues are *yours*. Your boundary issues? Yours. Your abandonment issues? Yours. Not your alcoholic father's. You have the power to work through them. You have the power to overcome them. And, how—boys and girls—do we do that? As always, *with love*! If you work up to having enough respect and love for yourself, then your issues *will not* be able to bring you down. Once you take ownership of your issues, you'll find yourself living more happily, successfully and freely than ever before. That's a big hurdle to overcome, you know. Meredith and Lexie, for example, have a *long* way to go. So, find comfort in the fact that you are *not* alone.

Of course, Meredith isn't the only person around here who has a habit of blaming mommy and daddy for many of her problems. She's just the most obvious. Let's see who else we have here . . .

Well, there's Cristina and her overbearing mother. Oh, yes, I believe her name is Helen. Helen, you see, has made several appearances at SGH. And, every last one of them has driven Cristina absolutely crazy! Way back when, Helen had quite a hand in Cristina's nervous breakdown. It was during the time of Cristina's ectopic pregnancy. You know the one. Well, the mere presence of her mother—her voice, her questions, her outfit— helped send Cristina over the edge. She was supposed to be recovering from her surgery. Instead, Cristina was wailing. Real tears, too. "Somebody sedate me!" she screamed. It was quite a scene, let me tell you.

More recently, Helen showed up to help Cristina plan her wedding. That must've been absolutely horrifying for the then-intern! I heard that Helen forced Cristina to try on one ghastly dress after another. Of course, Helen had a little bit of help . . . In the form of Burke's own mother—Mama Burke.

Let's just say that Cristina doesn't do well with mothers—hers *or* someone else's—period. However, to Cristina's credit, Burke's mom is in a class of mothers all her own. You certainly don't want to mess with Mama Burke! You see, Mama Burke was always skeptical of Cristina. She was just protecting her son, you know. It was clear that the elder Burke thought Cristina was way too selfish and way too focused on her career to make a proper wife for her baby boy. Although she tried, Cristina was never really able to get used to Mama Burke's overbearing nature. There's more coming up on all of that in our next chapter . . .

Undoubtedly, it hasn't been all mothers all the time at Seattle Grace. There have been a few fathers roaming the halls as well. You already know all about George's pop, Harold. But, I haven't yet mentioned Callie's dad . . . Another force to be reckoned with . . .

The senior Torres showed up one day, surprising both Callie and George. He was in town on business—yet—everybody knew he made a pit stop at SGH just to check out his daughter's husband. He took Callie and George to lunch at Joe's—where things didn't run so smoothly. George, you see, was hungover. As a matter of fact, for George, that day was *the day* . . . The day after he slept with Izzie. Oh, boy, poor Georgie must've been so out of it. Obviously, George couldn't get those thoughts of Izzie out of his head because he ended up nervously spilling his drink all over the table. He was pretty embarrassed. As was Callie.

You know, I wonder if Callie's father knows about his daughter's divorce. And I wonder if Callie's father knows George slept with another woman, *causing* that divorce. George better watch out—Callie's dad looked rather . . . intimidating. Scary. *Lethal.* Yep—George will *definitely* have some healing with love to do if Callie's dad ever comes back to town . . .

Okay—I want you to say the following sentence aloud, right now: "My past does not define me." Say it! "My past does not define me." I can't hear you! "My past does not define me!" Very good!

It's true, you know—the thing about your past not defining you.

So, daddy picked the younger, brighter, shinier version of you. Don't name *that* as the reason why you kicked McDreamy out of your bed. Don't name *that* as the reason why you won't let the perfect man love you. Wanna know what the real reason is? It's because you're not properly healing with love . . .

You need to forget about the past and what happened to you when you were five years old. Hey, if you're clutching the past to your chest so tightly, then how will you ever open up your arms and embrace the future? *You're* in the driver's seat. *You're* in control of your life. *Choose* to live better.

Here's the thing: Parents—mothers and fathers alike—will always examine their kids for signs of improvement. That's kind of *their job*. It doesn't have to be *your problem*. The next time your Alzheimer's-afflicted mother has a lucid day, comes into the hospital and acts all disappointed in you, refrain from giving her the satisfaction of knowing you really care what she has to say. Instead, *choose* to think positively. *Choose* to be issue-free. *Choose* to love! If you make those decisions, then it's absolutely impossible for world-famous-surgeon-mommy to make you doubt all of your future aspirations, dreams and desires . . . And, once you start focusing on *those* kinds of things instead of the hate-filled tirade your mother is spewing at you—I can guarantee you— you'll be infinitely happier.

CHAPTER SIXTEEN

Get Over It! Seriously!

*"By letting it go it all gets done. The world is won by
those who let it go. But when you try and try,
the world is beyond the winning."*

—LAO TZU,
philosopher

B Y NOW, I'M hoping you know that one of the most basic
and vital forms of healing with love is "letting go." Now,
although it's one of the most elementary practices of my philosophy, letting go is also one of the most difficult . . . Letting go
of what happened to you when you were five . . . Letting go of
the man who jilted you at the altar . . . Letting go of the husband who cheated on you by sleeping with his best friend . . .
Letting go of the boyfriend who—yesterday—was making out
with a scrub nurse, and—today—is building your dream house . . .
I'm telling you, letting go ain't so easy!

However, no matter how hard letting go can be, sometimes
it's absolutely essential. When you think about it, that's what life
is really all about . . . Knowing when to hold on and when to let
go. It's a delicate balance between the two. We have to use our
best judgment and listen to our inside voices in order to achieve
this equilibrium.

So how, then, do we let go? How, exactly, do we muster up
enough strength and courage to say goodbye to the detrimental

people in our lives? How do we part with our past? How do we forgive and forget? Well, the answers to those questions may lie in analyzing how NOT to let go. Uh oh, I'm sensing a pop quiz coming on . . . Oh, well, would you look below—I was right!

Which of the following is NOT an example of letting go?

A. Giving away the mixmasters, waffle makers and other gifts you received after your wedding that never happened.
B. Deciding to see other people when your girlfriend freezes up every time you mention marriage, commitment, a house and/or a future together.
C. Throwing your wedding ring into the Sound after realizing it's just bad juju.
D. Making your adulterous ex-husband, who happens to *still* be an intern while *you're* Chief Resident, pay for the errors of his ways by giving him torturous scut work—such as making him hold onto a wedding dress all day long.
E. Cooking breakfast for your half-sister—the one who used to stalk you, the one your man referred to as "the girl from the bar" and the one who Daddy picked.

Contestants, make your selection *now*.

The correct answer is . . . Ready? Okay . . . "D."

Yes, answers "A," "B," "C" and "E" are all wonderful examples of a person *letting go*. Choice "D," however, is not. You see, the situation I described in choice "D" is the only situation where someone continues to cling to pain. *That's* certainly not letting go. It might be called revenge, but it's definitely not called letting go. You're still wasting energy—*negative energy*—on the person you're trying to forget. And that's not going to help the matter at hand. Just ask my good, dear friend, Callie.

You're already familiar with the Callie-George-Izzie deal. Well, after Callie found out about George's faux pas, she seized the opportunity at revenge (at the advice of Mark, of course). Here's what happened . . .

A local bridal shop was holding an insane contest: Be the last woman holding onto a wedding dress and win the wedding of your dreams! Well, the competition left two women standing (sorta). One had a dislocated shoulder. The other had a whole slew of facial lacerations, a bloody nose and a chunk of missing scalp. Naturally, they were both brought to Seattle Grace . . . *still* clutching that wedding dress!

Those women wanted to win—badly. Both absolutely refused to let go of that wedding dress. One of the women required surgery for her injuries. But she just wouldn't let go, even though she needed an operation and time was of the essence! So Callie made George hold the dress *for* the injured woman. That way, the woman was still participating in the contest while she was undergoing surgery . . . And George was enduring humiliation.

It was really Mark's idea. But, it was Callie who put the plan into action. Ah, revenge. You know, Callie was *supposed* to enjoy torturing George—at least a little bit. However, she soon realized that revenge was futile. Making George hold a wedding dress all day wasn't going to change anything from her past. She was still a divorcee. She was still struggling as Chief Resident. She was still *exhausted*. Callie quickly discovered that hating George and finding ways to seek revenge upon him were just going to make her even more exhausted. So, she forgave him. And—as I've said before—forgiveness really is the best revenge anyway.

Callie completely wrote George off at that point. No more feelings. No more torture. No more energy wasted on George whatsoever. *That*, my friends, is called letting go.

Separately, I heard that George and Izzie decided to do a little letting go of their own rather recently, as well . . .

From what I could gather, their one night of passion meant a
lot more to George and Izzie than they could have ever imag-
ined. After that steamy—albeit drunken—evening, the pair de-
bated as to what to do next. Should George tell Callie? Izzie
thought so . . . But George thought differently. Telling Callie
was only going to hurt her. George assured Izzie that what they
did would never, *ever* happen again. Thus, Callie didn't need to
know . . .

Izzie and George soon began to grow apart. It was George
who tried to avoid Izzie, half ashamed, half worried that Callie
would find out. Izzie, on the other hand, began to truly miss her
best friend. George had *always* been there for her. When the
adoptive parents of Izzie's daughter came into the hospital one
day, it was George who consoled her. You see, Hannah—that's
the little girl Izzie had to give up after she became pregnant as a
teenager—had leukemia and was in desperate need of a bone
marrow transplant. After Hannah's initial donor died, Izzie became the only viable bone marrow donor for her little girl . . .

That was certainly an emotional day for Izzie, particularly after Hannah refused to meet her mother face to face. The little
girl simply wasn't ready yet. It was a hard pill for Izzie to swallow.
Still, she agreed to donate the marrow anyway. Luckily, George
was by Izzie's side the entire time, helping her through the excru-
ciating procedure. After the operation, George took Izzie down
to see her daughter receive her infusion. That little girl—let me
tell you—was beautiful. And, you know what was equally beautiful? Hannah receiving the wonderful gift that Izzie gave to her.

I believe that was the point when Izzie finally realized that
she couldn't do without George's friendship. Izzie's feelings for
her best friend were growing stronger and stronger by the day.

So, when George announced that he would be transferring to Mercy West, Izzie was devastated. She was about to lose her best friend for good.

You know, one of the scrub nurses told me a rather "interesting" thing she saw happen one day. She told me she was walking down the hallway, delivering labs, when the doors to a nearby elevator opened, revealing Izzie and George inside, standing in an *awkward* position. *Awkward* because Callie was standing directly in front of the elevator, glaring at the pair. *Awkward* because it *so* looked like George and Izzie had just been kissing. Yes—*awkward!* And, considering how everything seemed to work out, I wouldn't be surprised if Izzie and George were full-on making out in that elevator. Maybe Izzie hoped that a kiss would get George to stay at SGH? I'm not really sure. But it did seem like George had made up his mind . . .

In the end, whether because of Izzie or not, George decided to stay at Seattle Grace. And after a long second first day as an intern, George showed up at Izzie's door and finally professed his love. Yes, the best friends *were in love*. The only thing left to do, at that point, was to tell Callie. And, well, you know from Chapter Nine how *that* went down.

So, with Callie finally in the know (and everyone at SGH completely weirded out by the situation), George and Izzie were free to be together. *At last*. The friends-turned-lovers, however, soon realized that *something* felt off. Yeah—I heard the sex was *really* bad. Historically bad. Izzie's-box-of-fun bad. Just . . . *bad*.

The pair began to doubt their relationship. Sure, they gave romance a shot, but it just didn't seem to be enough. Yes, maybe Izzie and George were better as friends—and *not* lovers. The duo wrestled with their feelings for quite some time, but eventually admitted that the chemistry between them just wasn't there. So, they let go. In effect, they let go of each other.

Here's something else about this whole letting go thing: It takes love. You see, lots and lots of love is necessary to let someone *or something* go. And, by now you surely know that love allows you to heal. So, logically, if you're able to let go, then you're able to heal.

Izzie and George truly cared for one another. They didn't want to prolong the embarrassment or pain of their relationship any longer. So, they let go. It needed to be done. In order to heal from what they did to Callie *and* themselves, George and Izzie needed to let everything go . . . And they did.

Of course, "letting go" comes in many forms, as this chapter's quiz has illustrated. Letting go of the resentment toward your half-sister by making eggs for her, letting go of a failed marriage by hurling your wedding rings into the sea, letting go of a failed marriage attempt by giving away your wedding presents. Yes, there's no one way to let go. The possibilities are endless!

I, for one, had my eye on Cristina's waffle maker from the get go. It's true—after Burke abandoned her at the altar, Cristina dealt with her emotions (and anger) by auctioning off her gifts. And, let me tell you, those were some good gifts! Unfortunately, Nurse Tyler had more bargaining power than me and ended up scoring the Belgian Flip Round Pro, the lucky devil!

Mama Burke came into the hospital that day, searching for Cristina. Naturally, the moment Cristina saw Mrs. Burke, she ducked for cover! Well, sneaky Nurse Tyler used the situation for his own advantage. He could either tell Mama Burke exactly where Cristina was, *or* he could do Cristina a favor and pretend he didn't know. That favor, of course, would cost Cristina her amazing waffle maker. So what was it going to be? Confronting Mama Burke? Or giving Tyler the gift? It was all up to Cristina. I bet you know what she did . . .

Surprisingly, however, Cristina was able to hide from Mama

Burke the *entire* day. Some of Cristina's co-workers weren't so lucky. Yes, Mama Burke used her evil ways to get into the minds of Meredith, George and Derek before she finally got her chance to speak to Cristina. It turned out that Mrs. Burke wasn't there to pity or confront Cristina, as suspected. No, Mrs. Burke was there to get the key to Cristina's apartment so that she could gather her son's things. Moreover, Mama also wanted the necklace that she had previously given Cristina to wear in her wedding . . . The wedding that didn't happen.

You know, I was never invited to that wedding. Not that I expected to be. Cristina and I were never bff's or anything like that . . . Anyway, I suppose I didn't miss much now, did I? Oh, sure, there were the lovely (and uncomfortable) bridesmaids— Izzie and Callie—who both worried about George's whereabouts. There was the tortured maid of honor—Meredith—who seemed to put an end to her own relationship with the agonizing best man—Derek—when she muttered, "It's over. It's so over." And, of course, there were the distressed bride and groom—Cristina and Burke . . . Oh, Cristina and Burke . . .

Their relationship was really headed toward disaster ever since Burke proposed. You see, Cristina had never been "the marrying type." She'd be the first one to tell you that she was a surgeon, *not* a wife. So, when Burke got down on one knee and whispered those magical words, Cristina was speechless . . . literally. She didn't say "yes." She didn't say "no" either. Instead, she said the proposal was "under advisement." Reluctantly, though, in Cristina's own little way, she agreed to marry Burke. But, she didn't do rings . . . She didn't really care about the flavor of her cake . . . And, there definitely wasn't going to be any mosquito-netted veil covering her face on the big day.

Well, when that big day finally arrived, Cristina was—in fact— *a mess.* She had written her vows down—on her hand—but seemed to have wiped them off when she scrubbed in for surgery. From what I heard, Cristina was about to lose it. Thankfully, Meredith stepped in and gave her a little pep talk. Something about happy endings . . .

Meanwhile, Burke stood at the altar, patiently waiting for Cristina to open the doors and walk down the aisle. But it looked like Cristina wasn't coming. And Burke was done waiting. He found Cristina just outside the doors . . . plucked eyebrows and all. Cristina said she was ready. In his heart, however, Burke knew that she wasn't . . .

Burke told Cristina that if he truly loved her, he would set her free. If he truly loved her, Burke wouldn't be making Cristina do something she very clearly didn't want to do . . . If he truly loved her, he would let her go. So he did.

Burke, my dears, was healing with love. Remember what I told you earlier? Letting go takes love! Burke, you see, was done. That day, he left the church, Cristina and Seattle Grace behind . . . never to return again.

Cristina, of course, had her breakdown soon after. Rumor has it that, when she got home, Cristina stood in her Burke-less apartment, in her wedding gown, and completely let her emotions run wild. It's good to do that, sometimes. To just let it all out. To just let it all go. I imagine, at that particular moment in time, that even Cristina herself didn't know if she was crying because of Burke's hasty exit or because she allowed someone to change her.

That's what Burke did, you see. He changed Cristina. I mean, there was Cristina—not in pretty blue scrubs—but in a *wedding dress* of all things. There was Cristina with plucked eyebrows, wearing a necklace that was literally cutting off her circulation. There was the former strong, focused and emotionless Cristina who was now bawling and wailing over her happy ending gone sour. A changed Cristina indeed.

Which brings me back to the wedding gifts . . . One of Cristina's very first attempts at letting it all go. As they say, letting go is a lot like crossing monkey bars . . . You've got to let go in order to move forward.

The thing is, plans change. It's something you just have to accept. You may not spend the rest of your life with the man you married at the Church of Elvis in Vegas. You won't necessarily have the chemistry you thought you'd have with the best friend you thought you fell in love with. You might not make it down the aisle on your wedding day. And, likewise, you may not live happily ever after with your McDreamy. Currently, Meredith is wrestling with that last thought as I type these very words . . .

A few weeks ago, Meredith and Derek had a fight. Now, I know what you're thinking: big deal! It's true, it wasn't the first time Meredith and Derek had an argument. But, there was something about this quarrel that made me question whether they were finally letting go of one another for good. Sad, but *true* . . .

The latest drama culminated over a little scrub nurse named Rose. Apparently, Derek and Rose locked lips not too long ago. Well, this Rose ain't such an innocent little flower now, is she?

Derek and Rose met—where else—in the OR. During surgery on a teenaged boy, Derek remarked that he was glad to be out of high school. All of those miserable cliques. Well, Nurse Rose couldn't help but let out a little giggle. Derek asked what was funny and Rose responded—Seattle Grace is just as cliquey, if not more, than high school! After all, Rose had worked on 36 of Derek's surgeries, and *that* was the first time McDreamy noticed. Yeah—talk about cliques!

Derek and Rose's friendship quickly blossomed. It didn't take long before Derek was pointing out licorice in Rose's teeth and noticing the engagement ring she wore around her neck.

Yep—Rose had once been engaged. But the engagement was eventually called off. See, whereas Rose knew exactly what she wanted, her fiancé did not. Obviously, it struck a chord with Derek. He knows what he wants, too; it's Meredith who doesn't . . .

Sure enough, another nurse witnessed the two kissing in the scrub room after a successful surgery. Derek had just saved a life and Rose had just fixed a broken machine in the middle of the operation. The two were exhilarated and energized—so, they kissed. The snooping nurse said it was a nice kiss—nothing major. Still, it was a kiss.

Meanwhile, a little drama had been building between Meredith and Derek for quite some time. Derek was getting fed up with Mer's lack of commitment (see Chapter Six). He wanted to marry Meredith. He wanted to build her a home. He wanted to share a life with her. Derek would tell all of this to Meredith, but— Meredith being Meredith—would freeze up every time. Meredith didn't know what she wanted. So, how was Derek supposed to build a future with her? Still—McDreamy being McDreamy—he pressed on . . .

Derek brought a set of blueprints into the hospital to show Meredith. The plans were for his dream home—*their* dream home. You know, the one that Meredith and Derek would share *together*. Meredith, of course, tried to act cool, but—everybody could tell—she was frightened. Then, George accidentally let it slip that he heard Derek had kissed Rose. And, well, let's just say that Meredith was *not* a happy camper!

Yes, Seattle Grace's most contentious couple had a *huge* fight . . . For all of the hospital to see and hear. Meredith was furious that Derek was making out with a scrub nurse yesterday and planning their dream house today. Derek was upset because he knew—he just *knew*—that Meredith would find some reason to walk away after seeing those plans. It goes all the way back to Mer's fear of commitment and abandonment issues. The argument even came full circle when Meredith brought up the fact that it was Derek who never told her that he was married to Addison. Remember that one? Oh, boy, that's never good . . . Yes—Meredith admitted that she was *never* able to trust Derek. So, Derek said he was done. As was Meredith.

And . . . that night . . . Derek was seen leaving the hospital with none other than . . . Rose!

So, what does this mean? What does this mean?! Have Meredith and Derek finally decided to let one another go? I'm not sure—but if Meredith and Derek are causing one another as much pain as I think, then maybe it *is* time for them to part ways. Perhaps Meredith and Derek's time to truly let go of one another is *long overdue* . . .

As I want to make very clear, "letting go" doesn't mean "giving up." Rather, "letting go" means accepting that there are some things that simply can't be. Like Callie and George. Like Izzie and George. Like Addison and Derek. And, as we may soon discover, even like Meredith and Derek.

So here's the deal: Letting go is about acceptance and it's about *love*. It's about admitting there are some things—no matter how bad you think you want them—that simply cannot be attained. Like I said, plans change. Ten years ago, if you had asked me where I would be today, chances are I would've told you that I'd be the Chief Resident of a cutting-edge hospital somewhere in Seattle. I'd be married. I might even be pregnant. Well, *none* of those things have happened for me. And, that's just something I've had to learn to accept. For my own good! Because, if I had refused to let those plans go, then I would've never been able to join the likes of Louisa May Alcott, Virginia Woolf and Kate Chopin (to name just a few) by carefully constructing this very book, destined to be enjoyed by generations to come.

Therefore, "letting go" allows you to forge ahead. It allows you to become stronger, wiser and—ultimately—happier. It allows you to love. As you know, loving allows you to heal. By letting go, you can get over your past, your partner or even your half-sister who really has nothing to do with your abandonment issues. So, it's up to you! I will leave you with this, though: Living in the past is unhealthy! You'll never be able to go back and make a brand new start. It's up to you whether you want to start now and make a brand new ending. Choose to forge ahead, my comrades. Choose to use the tools I've taught you and choose to heal with love . . .

HERONISM

In order to let go, you need to decide what you want. You see, realizing what you want—and, in effect, what you *don't* want—makes it easier to let go of certain things. A "vision board" is something that can assist you through this oftentimes confusing process.

A "vision board" is literally a board where you can place text, pictures and objects that describe or symbolize your goals. It's a collage of dreams! And, it's a beautiful thing! Cut out pictures of the things you want from books and magazines. Write down your favorite words, quotes and phrases. Draw illustrations of the things you want, too. Remember, you're collecting things that make you—and only you—truly happy. Add all of them to your vision board.

When you're done (keep in mind, you don't *ever* have to actually be done), put your board in a place where you'll see it every day. When you do see it, take a moment to really look at it. It's okay to get excited about it!

Now, if you're ever having a hard time letting go of something, take a look at your vision board. Is the "someone" or "something" you're trying to let go of preventing you from achieving anything on that board? If so, then that's even *more* reason to let that "someone" or "something" go! Good luck!

Epilogue:
Loving Yourself—Dead or Alive

"It is never too late to be who you might have been."

—GEORGE ELIOT

MEET NORMAN. The world's oldest intern. Just your average fella who—in his mid sixties—had a change of heart and decided he wanted to become a surgeon. True story! After transferring to SGH from UCLA, Norman was given to—of all people—Alex. Surprisingly, the sprightly intern was able to handle *all* of resident Alex Karev's disparaging remarks with poise and grace. He didn't seem to care what others thought about him—those *ageists*. In *my* opinion, Norman fit right in around here—right down to the T-shirt he wore underneath his scrubs and his use of the commonly used phrase, "Seriously." He never let his bum hip or arthritis cream get in the way of his work, which—at his age—was quite admirable.

In short, Norman was a real sweetheart, let me tell you. More importantly, however, Norman was a shining example of someone who completely and totally accepted himself. Oh, yes, when it came to self-acceptance, well, Norman could've written the book! (Lucky for me, he didn't.)

You see, Norman set a goal. And, with unwavering motivation

and drive, Norman set out to achieve it. Along the way, he broke through barriers, surpassed his limitations and overcame hurdles. He listened to the voice inside his head. Norman *never* took his eyes off the prize. You know why? Because Norman loved himself. He loved who he was and who he was going to become—a doctor! This, my lovelies, is what self-acceptance is really all about: truly loving every single part of yourself—so that *nothing* is able to stop you from following your dreams.

Once you start accepting and loving yourself, not only will you be able to set goals, but you'll be able to achieve them as well. Look at it this way . . . You take good care of the things you love, right? Well, then, follow your dreams and make stepping stones out of stumbling blocks . . . That's how I want you to take good care of the thing you're supposed to love most: yourself.

Norman is living proof that it's *never* too late to start loving yourself. And, when I say never, I mean *never*. You know what—let's capitalize, italicize and underline *NEVER*. Because I mean it's *NEVER* too late for you to invest in some good, old-fashioned self-love. Oh, what's that? You want *more* proof? Proof *beyond* the living? Okay, then—it's never too late to start loving yourself . . . *even if you're dead*. Ha! Is that you laughing over there? You think that's funny? Well, it's not. Just ask Meredith . . .

Remember that big ferry crash I told you about? Well, during the chaos, as she tended to an injured man on the ferry docks, Meredith was accidentally knocked into the freezing cold water. She was actually missing for quite some time. Derek eventually realized that Meredith must've gone under—so he dove in to search for his lover. I know . . . How romantic, right? Anyway, Derek soon found Mer's lifeless body floating underneath the Sound. Terrified, Derek lifted Meredith up out of the water and brought her back to Seattle Grace. But, it was too late . . . Meredith flatlined.

It's true. Meredith was dead. Cold, blue and dead. I remember passing Addison standing in the hallway outside of Meredith's room. She was completely stunned. She looked almost as lifeless as Meredith did. Cristina, Izzie, Alex and George were trying to hold it together as well. And, as for Derek . . . Oh, poor Derek. He wanted to help in any way he could. But, there was simply nothing he could do, except wait. Like everybody else. Yes, it was a tragic day at Seattle Grace.

Meanwhile, inside Meredith's room, a team of doctors worked furiously to bring Meredith back to life. Richard, Burke and Bailey—the looks on their faces didn't seem too reassuring. Clearly, their efforts weren't going so well.

I was mostly in the clinic that day—just offering my support and comforting the loved ones of the *many* people who went missing in the crash. It was an insanely tense and stressful place. At times, even us doctors lost our cool. Callie, for instance, totally snapped at me! But, that's neither here nor there . . . I remained focused on the job at hand. Then, I overheard someone say that Meredith *still* hadn't woken up. Oh, boy, that wasn't good . . .

I remained positive, however. Said a little prayer. Mer was probably just in some white void, talking to people like Denny and bomb expert Dylan. She was probably surrounded by cheerful dead people. Maybe Bonnie, the train wreck/pole impalement patient, was there. Or, perhaps Liz, Ellis' old scrub nurse, had been keeping Meredith company this whole time. And Doc the dog had to be there, too! Yes, I tried to think happy thoughts—Meredith was simply at a happy family reunion of sorts, chock full of happy dead people. You know, just . . . happy.

As Meredith continued to lie lifeless, her mother happened to be just a few doors down—clinging to her own life. Ellis had already been in the hospital for a few days and was about to undergo heart surgery. I heard that Derek, without anything else to do except worry about Meredith, went into Ellis' room where he had a little "talk" with the senior Grey. Emotional and a bit unstable, Derek began to blame Ellis for everything wrong with Meredith—her abandonment issues, her mommy issues, her daddy issues, her fear of commitment. Ellis, in Derek's opinion, ruined Meredith. And, it was a miracle that Meredith survived . . . *despite* her mother.

Although it *probably* had nothing to do with Derek's tongue-lashing (no one knows for sure), Ellis went into cardiac arrest moments after Derek had left. Derek rushed back in to save Ellis. He intubated. He defibrillated. He shocked her—time and time again—but, there was no use . . . Ellis flatlined. Ellis died.

Well, it seems that miracles really *do* happen, because—at the exact moment Ellis died—Meredith woke up. Now, whether Ellis' passing was related to her daughter's living, well, the jury's out on that one! From *this* point of view, however, I'd wager that the two happenings were indeed directly related. I wouldn't be surprised if Meredith saw her mother walking toward her in the afterlife and that—in and of itself—was enough to scare the crap out of the poor girl and make her jump back to the land of the living!

Look, you already know all about Meredith's issues. Although *we*—as in, you and I—know that Ellis can't be blamed for everything wrong with Meredith (see Chapter Fifteen), Meredith, on the other hand, does not. With Ellis joining her in that creepy white void, Meredith realized that she had to *fight* to escape. Perhaps it was even Ellis herself that told Mer she needed to do so. Whatever the case may be, Meredith realized that she had a whole lot more living (and loving) left to do. If her mother—the person she held responsible for *all* of her issues—were really gone, then maybe Meredith could finally live happily ever after . . . The only thing she needed to do, then, was fight. So, Meredith fought. She used her tiny, ineffectual fists—that now looked blue—to fight for a new life. And, she woke up.

Yes, Meredith had to literally *die* in order to make that first step toward self-acceptance. It was there in that void where Meredith realized she needed to fight in order to stay above water. It was there in that void where Meredith realized her intimacy issues were so, so *stupid*. It was there in that void where Meredith realized she was anything but ordinary. Equipped with all of that knowledge, Meredith began accepting herself. That's proof—beyond the living—that it's *NEVER* too late to start loving yourself.

Afterward, a new and improved Meredith roamed the halls of Seattle Grace. She became more positive! She started painting with all the colors of the wind! She believed that "people are what matters." Dog gone it, I'd say Meredith was healing with love!

Of course—Mer wasn't perfect just yet. She still clung to many of her issues. She was still haunted by Ellis (that is, until Mer finally got rid of her mother's ashes—down the scrub room drain and back to the sea). But, as we all know, healing with love is a *journey*, not a destination. At least Meredith had gotten herself on the right path. And it only took dying to do so! Clearly, that just goes to show that self-acceptance is a tremendous challenge!

Now, I don't highly recommend dying as a way to rediscover yourself. It's not very safe and should only be attempted by trained professionals (at Seattle Grace Hospital). My dear friend Norman's method of choice for self-acceptance is *much* more preferred . . . That is, set a goal, then work fervently to reach that goal. And don't take your eyes off of that prize, my friends.

You will, of course, encounter hurdles along the way. However, keep in mind that life's problems were called hurdles because there's always a way to get over them. You'll soon discover that this approach breeds self-love, which ultimately leads to self-acceptance. And, wow. Just . . . *wow*. You're really healing with love now.

Take a moment to ask yourself where you currently stand in your own personal heal with love journey. Go on—give it a good five minutes. I'll be here when you come back . . .

Okay, great. So, I'm dying to know! *Where are you?* I have a feeling you're standing at one of the following locations, just like my colleagues.

Are you . . .

At a crossroads? Are you deciding whether McDreamy is really *McDreamy*? Is he actually "the one"? Was he kissing a scrub nurse yesterday and building your dream house today? Do you not trust him? Have you realized that you've *never* been able to trust him? Oh, sweetie, you have to let go in order to move forward. Maybe the time to do so is long overdue. Maybe, then, you'll be *really* ready to commit. Maybe you'll *actually* be ready to move in with him! At any rate, those are questions *you and only you* can answer . . .

At a point where you've begun to realize that your lady friend just isn't ready? Well, perhaps Meredith will *never* be ready. Her issues—they seem to be way too much to handle nowadays. Are you about to throw in the towel and *finally* let go, too? It's okay, you know. It's okay if you've chosen to grab a bite to eat with Rose. Lots of people are going to be mad at you, but it's okay because it'll just give you one more thing to heal from . . .

Currently in the middle of a competition? You're competing for Dr. Hahn's service. You've already picked your specialty: *cardio* all the way, baby. The problem is, cardio goddess Hahn doesn't like you. Well, you've certainly got a lot to prove. But, be careful . . . Don't try *too* hard . . .

Thinking you've got something *different* to offer? You're a people person. You're sympathetic. You're able to put yourself in other people's shoes quite easily. Cristina's got *nothing* on you. You're just as good as her! The race for cardio and Hahn's service? *It's on.* Just be sure to maintain respect for your opponent and try not to get too wrapped up in the competition . . .

Ooh—Suffering because Mom just paid you a visit? And, what's that? You *never* told her you divorced your wife? Mom raised you better, Catholic boy. I bet you're on the verge of making some positive life changes and that's really swell! I do think you need to start that change *now,* though. And, do it flamboyantly (but, you know, not *too* flamboyantly). Maybe you need a change of scenery . . . Maybe you need a new place to live . . . Maybe you need to become a resident (finally) . . .

Realizing you've recently gone through one change too many? Found out your husband was cheating on you, got a divorce, lost your job as Chief Resident . . . Girl, I think stability is just what the doctor ordered for *you*! You need a good friend. You need somebody you can relate to—somebody that shares your disinterest in the human race . . .

Hahn? Is that you over there? You're working. You're impressing the Chief and keeping your interns busy. You're all work and no play, I say! You could certainly use a good friend. Somebody to accompany to Joe's . . . Perhaps you need to ease up on Mark the manwhore. He's not all bad, you know. Just go back and reread Chapter Eleven. A little fun *might* do you some good . . .

Don't get too excited, manwhore. Hahn isn't giving you the

goods . . . You are just at the beginning of your journey. As a matter of fact, have you even started? Well, you certainly have *a lot* of work left to do. Stop trying so hard to prove that you're a man of substance. Remember—self-acceptance is the key. I'd suggest setting some kind of goal—something other than bedding Hahn . . .

And then there's *you*. Sleeping with your friend's half-sister by day . . . Sleeping with the Jane Doe you saved—who happens to be married—by night. You're a mess. But at least you own it. This is quite a predicament you've gotten yourself into. You're a real MIT. That is, manwhore-in-training. You do have time to turn your life around, you know. Remember, it's never too late to start loving yourself . . .

Which leaves you, standing there—*confused*—on your journey. Am I right? You went to Alex for sex. Now you found out about good ol' Jane Doe. Well, what'd you expect? At least things with your half-sister are going well . . . I think you could benefit from a change of scenery, too. You need a new place to live, too . . .

Are you sitting there—in the residents' lounge—playing the other day's events over and over again in your head? Somebody— maybe even you—left the baby gate open and a horrific accident ensued. Alas, your baby survived. But, your marriage is treading water right now. You're going to have to forgive yourself before you can even think about forgiving your husband . . . Keep in mind, we all make mistakes . . . I truly hope you can find at least *some* solace in that . . .

And, finally, we're left with you . . . At a junction where you've determined, although you've got your hands full, you're actually doing pretty well! I salute you. Not too long ago, you recognized your mistakes. You vowed to learn from them. You made a decision to do it all over again. Well, congratulations,

Chief, you're doing it! You're living. You're loving. You're healing. Keep up the good work. And, continue to be there for those who need the help.

I want you to now think back to the day you decided to pick up this book. Your complicated problems, your horrible fears, your sad worries—remember those? Well—have any of them now become *less* complicated? *Less* horrible? A tiny bit *less* sad? Well, it's my sincere hope that you can answer that question with a resounding, "Yes!" Oh, you can?! Well, congratulations! That means you're healing with love! And, that means my master plan worked!

It may come as a surprise to you, but I've been secretly instilling my very own loving way (patent pending) into your subconscious mind since Chapter One. Yes—through a series of carefully calculated principles, objectives, examples and declarations, I've rewired your brain and altered your attitude in order to make you willing to let go of the past, turn your attention to the future and heal with love.

So, some of my critics will call it brainwashing. I, on the other hand, will beg to differ. First of all, I wrote this book for your own good! Second, this isn't *Close Encounters of the Third Kind.* You haven't been abducted. I'm not some strange life form you've stumbled across on your journey. No one has been "brainwashing" you, per se. You've just been acquiring the extraordinary tools necessary to get yourself out of any and every kind of personal rut. As you're well aware, that's called healing with love.

Isn't it a great feeling? Knowing that you're equipped with the knowledge to turn any situation into a positive one? Knowing that—if you wanted—you can win the race for Chief! You can muster up enough strength to let go of the people and things you truly need to let go of! You can become the next cardio god-dess! You can survive your boyfriend's death! You can forgive your husband and yourself for that whole baby gate fiasco! You can get over your divorce! You don't have to be a manwhore! You don't have to blame Mommy for kicking McDreamy out of your bed, either!

Oh, I'm like a proud mama right now—I could go on and on, listing the things you can do with your newfound philosophy. But, I'll stop there because I don't want to take up any more of your time. Yes, I realize your time is precious. After all, that's time you could be using to love in the present moment and say buh-bye to stinkin' thinkin'. It's time you could be using to ap-preciate your friends and cheer on your new way of thinking. It's time you could be using to hug it out! And I *certainly* don't want to keep you from doing any of that!

Yes, my little students, the time to heal with love is *now*. So what are you waiting for? Put the book down! Show me—and the rest of the world—what you got!

I'll see you on the other side!

> *With All My Love,*
> *Sydney*

PART FOUR

The Healing with Love Quiz

Healing with Love—
The Official Quiz

Y OU'VE READ THE CHAPTERS. You've learned the principles. You've practiced the Heronisms. Now, it's time for you to sharpen those number two pencils, hunker down and take the official Healing with Love Quiz!

That's right, it's Test Day! I wish I could offer each and every one of you some of my freshly baked chocolate chip cookies, but I can't. You're on your own now. I know—we've certainly been through a lot together, but this is where we part ways. *I* have to go back to my duties at Seattle Grace. And, *you* have to go out into the world and heal with love. The following test will send you on your way. Let's find out if you're ready . . .

Remember: You can do this. *You can do this.* Good luck!

1. What is the most common mistake made by healing with love beginners?

   A. The transcontinental booty call.
   B. Seeking revenge on your cheating intern of a husband.

    C. Thinking negatively (i.e., embracing the term "Code Black").

    D. Healing with too much love (i.e., having a one night stand).

2. "Pink mist" is:

    A. Synonymous with "Code Black."

    B. Stinkin' thinkin'.

    C. Flecks of human flesh and blood, often caused by a bomb-in-a-body-cavity explosion.

    D. All of the above.

3. What is the most glorious, most beautiful blessing of all?

    A. Being somebody's person.

    B. McSteamy in a towel.

    C. Winning the race for Chief.

    D. Elevator rides with McDreamy.

4. Which of the following is the *best* way to become a cheerleader of love?

    A. Sleeping with your best friend.

    B. Going on a date with a handsome neurosurgeon.

    C. Pounding six shots of tequila.

    D. Acting as wingman and introducing the Chief to some "ladies."

5. Failed your intern test? Well, then:

    A. Transfer to Mercy West.

    B. Tell your wife you slept with a supermodel-turned-doctor.

C. Hug it out.

D. Get a haircut.

6. Your McDreamy just unveiled his plans for your dream house. Which of the following statements should be your response?

A. "I already *have* a house."

B. "This is a lot. This is a lot and this is really fast and this is . . ." <run>

C. "Yesterday you were kissing a scrub nurse and today you're building our dream house?"

D. "A big, beautiful house with kids' bedrooms and French doors and three and a half baths? Yes, yes, yes and YES!"

7. If you strive for perfection instead of excellence, you:

A. Are a robot.

B. Are healing with love.

C. Will perform many intricate surgeries, even with a hand tremor.

D. Will impress the Chief.

8. What is the *best* thing you can do for your relationship?

A. Tell the truth.

B. "Key" your partner.

C. Build a dream house together.

D. Wear a nose strip if you snore.

9. After discovering your husband's affair with a former supermodel, you should:

A. Seek revenge.

B. Cafeteria. Noon. You and your husband's skank. Be there.

C. Take your rage out on a patient.

D. Ultimately decide to let it go.

10. "Karma" means:

A. Poison oak where nobody wants to get poison oak.

B. Bad sex.

C. Putrid goo all over your pretty blue scrubs.

D. All of the above.

11. Which of the following is the *most appropriate* use of rejection?

A. Telling the world-renowned neonatal surgeon that you just slept with, "You're not my girlfriend, okay?"

B. Advising the Jane Doe patient you like to "stick with the decent guy."

C. Visiting a friend in another state to rejuvenate, recharge and relax.

D. Ordering another tequila shot and forgetting you were ever rejected in the first place.

12. For those who heal with love, which of the following is the *worst* thing to lose?

A. Your best friend.

B. A chance to get better.

C. Your potential soul mate.

D. The sixty-day sex bet.

13. If a man asks you if you want his pickle, you are dealing with:

   A. The ManWhore
   B. The Bad Boy
   C. The Perfectionist
   D. McDreamy

14. When communicating with a manwhore, always begin by:

   A. Admiring his physique.
   B. Making sure there are no witnesses nearby.
   C. Setting boundaries.
   D. Picturing him in that hand towel.

15. Your "healing with love journey" ends when:

   A. You stop feeling guilty about killing your fiancé.
   B. You're done lying on the bathroom floor.
   C. You find yourself in that great, white void with Denny and friends.
   D. Newsflash! Your healing with love journey *never* ends.

16. If you sometimes feel guilt and sorrow for your past actions, then:

   A. You're human and it's okay.
   B. You're living in the past and failing to embrace the future.
   C. You're still not ready to cash that eight million dollar check your lover left behind.
   D. You're pathetic—and will *never* learn to heal with love!

17. What should you do if, say, your father passed away at the hands of your colleagues?

   A. Unleash your rage and yell at your colleagues in the middle of the hospital.
   B. Realize they did everything they could and *forgive*.
   C. Go on a sexual rampage.
   D. Elope with your girlfriend to the Church of Elvis in Vegas.

18. Which of the following decisions is the *most* important?

   A. The decision between strawberry and chocolate ice cream.
   B. The decision between your wife and your hospital.
   C. The decision between surgeries and pony births.
   D. The decision to love.

19. What is the *worst* thing you can do during a competition?

   A. Change your strategy.
   B. Count your competitors' blessings.
   C. Remain committed to one-upping your opponents.
   D. End all personal relationships in an effort to stay focused.

20. Your "boundary issues" belong to:

   A. You.
   B. Your alcoholic father.
   C. Your adulterous mother.
   D. Your stalker half-sister.

21. True/False: To heal with love—Start immediately. Do it flamboyantly. No exceptions.

22. True/False: "Half-truths" are "whole lies."

23. True/False: If you're having trouble telling the truth to your boyfriend's ex-wife, morphine can be used as a *last resort*.

24. True/False: If you've cheated on your wife with your best friend, then you are *a cheater*.

25. True/False: It *is* possible for a manwhore to evolve into "a man of substance."

26. True/False: You turned into your mommy when you *decided* to turn into your mommy.

27. True/False: Letting go takes love.

28. True/False: If you truly love someone, you will *never* let that someone go.

29. True/False: In essence, "letting go" means "giving up."

30. True/False: Sometimes, it's necessary to literally *die* (as in—drowning in the Sound, remaining unconscious and visiting your dead friends in some big, scary white void) in order to take that first step toward self-acceptance.

ANSWERS

1. D	16. A
2. D	17. B
3. A	18. D
4. B	19. B
5. C	20. A
6. D	21. False
7. A	22. True
8. A	23. True
9. D	24. False
10. D	25. True
11. C	26. True
12. B	27. True
13. A	28. False
14. C	29. False
15. D	30. True